365 Questions Of The Day

Volume III

Robert Trajkovski

365 Questions Of The Day- Volume III

365 Questions of The Day

Copyright © 2014 by Robert Trajkovski

All rights reserved. No part of this book may be reproduced or transmitted in any form or by any means electronic, mechanical, photocopying, recording or by any information storage and retrieval systems without prior permission of the author except in the case of brief quotation in articles or reviews.

Cover design by Robert Trajkovski

Publisher RTCo.

ISBN 978-0983676379

www.365QOD.blogspot.com

E-mail: roberttrajkovski2010@yahoo.com

THANKS to the editor

---

and many loyal blog readers

Introduction-Updated for year 3

During the last three years I have been writing a daily blog called 365 Questions of the Day (365QOD). The blog can be found at: www.365QOD.blogspot.com

The daily posts have been based on topics of interest to me, books or articles I have read or was in the process of reading. In other words, the post topics are very random. However, I did assign a label for each post.

Imagine the last years' worth of posts as 365 random blots of color on a canvas. You can tell there are some similarities between the blots but the picture is not totally clear. The purpose of this book is to re-arrange these blots into a new picture where the posts are organized by label and each topic forms a chapter.

Before I reorganized the posts I decided to correct all of the posts. After my first edit my thought was that I should have just put all of the posts into a word document and published it. Keep It Simple Sweetheart. But I was not happy. I found too many mistakes. I wrote with passion but many posts were poorly written.

It was frustrating to go through the book a second and third time and find just as many mistakes. No excuse for writing so poorly. I really started to appreciate my loyal followers.

Just like any project, initially there is excitement and then the grind starts. Eventually one can see the end of the tunnel. I believe that after many edits that the book you are holding provides a much improved version of the blog posts.

I hope that the book is of use to you. It is very wide in the scope of topics. That is the intent of the blog: to improve the thinking by introducing new thoughts from various sources.

I urge you to read each section and to pause in order to think about it. In my opinion reading through the book would be fruitless.

I consider myself a work in progress. The book as it stands shows my thoughts during the third year of the blog existence. I am far from perfect, but I do consider myself on a journey to get better. Please join me.

Let me know your thoughts

Roberttrajkovski2010@yahoo.com

Table of Contents

Acceptance	9
Action	12
Balance	27
Belief	22
Ben	32
Brand	34
Business	42
Change	55
Communication	57
Connections	72
Creativity	77
Decision Making	93
Demanding	117
Direction	119
Doing	126
Entrepreneur	131
Exceeding	185
Fear	188
Feelings	194
Financial	196
Focus	204
Giving	211
Grit	213
Happiness	216
Influence	220
Leadership	225
Learning	231

Learning about others	248
Life Mission	254
Making Mistakes	261
Mastery	264
Memorable	268
Motivation	297
Passion	299
Persistence	305
PMP	308
Receiving	310
Result	312
Routine	314
Sources	323
Spiritual	325
Strategy	335
Stretching	351
Success	361
Success Intelligence	382
Teamwork	406
Transitions	413
Zen	415
Conclusion	424

Thursday, February 6, 2014

365QOD- Day1096

Before I start the post today I want to say THANKS...THANKS...THANKS for supporting me for three years in my writing endeavors.

Three Years of Focus

"Focus"- word my wife wrote in pencil on a wall next to my side of the bed

Three years ago on February 1, 2011 I started writing this blog. My wife's word was a spark. Another spark was reading Ka-Ching and wanting to apply it. These sparks have led me to continuously write a daily blog for each of the 1095=365*3 days.

Each year I try to reflect as to why I continue to write the posts. The funny thing is that my wife is now one of my biggest non-supporters. She thinks it is a waste of my time. I completely disagree.

My blog serves as a database of experiences, stories, and my thoughts on many subjects. It is me without too much being held back. I write about whatever catches my eye, makes me pause for a moment, or simply excites me. You can look at the topics and clearly see where my thoughts are directed towards:

acceptance, action, balance, belief,ben, brand, branding, business, celebrating, change, communicating, communication, communications, connections, creativity,   decision making, demanding, Direction, doing, entrepreneur, exceeding, fear,

feelings, financial, flow, focus, Franklin,giving, grit, happiness, I am,influence,   integrity, leadership, learning, learning about others, learning from others, life mission, making mistakes, mastery, memorable,

momentum, motivation, passion,persistence, PMP, procrastination, receiving,   result, r outine, sources,spiritual, strategy, stretching, success, success intelligence,teamwork, transitions, zen

Most of all, the blog allows me to fulfill my deepest need- to be creative each day. It is my drug of choice. I get a natural high from just stopping and writing a few paragraphs. Sometimes I will read an older post and immediately see the beauty that I tried to express.

The blog is also one of my biggest challenges. I am not a natural writer or editor. Most often I write quickly and do not do enough proof reading. When I sit down at the end of the year to put the book together I find it so frustrating that I did not catch 90+ percent of the mistakes.

However, I do believe that overall the quality and length are getting better. I do read the post most of the times before I hit publish. And naturally over time I have increased the length in order to improve the quality of the content. The numbers of readers are up so maybe I am succeeding?

Again, THANKS for your support and hopefully year four will be better than the first three combined. I will be working to make it worth your while to invest the time in reading it.

Today's question is:

"How do you make yourself to keep going for extended amount of time?"

Acceptance

Thursday, December 12, 2013

365QOD- Day1041
Stressed Out

"The **amygdalae** are almond-shaped groups of nuclei located deep and medially within the temporal lobes of the brain in complex vertebrates, including humans." - Wikipedia

I watched a special on PBS last night. They always show very cool stuff during their money drives. The special was called Mind Over Medicine. The author Dr. Lissa Rankin presented her views of how some things are not explainable with western medicine and we need to be aware of alternatives.

According to Rankin, the amygdala is supposed to shut off within 30 seconds of a life threatening event. An example of such an event is a situation in which a car almost hits you. The life threatening event lasts for a few seconds at best. Unfortunately, modern life stress causes the amygdala to stay active most of the time.

So how do you stop stressing? I read an article by Bahram Akradi in which he uses the following technique.
1. **"If the present is stressful, put your focus on the future."**
This makes sense. At times we do not have complete control of our present but we can clearly see where we are headed towards.

2. **"If the future is stressful, put your focus on the present."** Sometimes we know of events that will occur in the future. Just because we know what will happen it does not mean we know when or how. In those moments we should pull back and focus on what we can do now.

3. If 1 and 2 did not work for you then, **"If you're still stressed out, make a contingency plan."** This is when you take out a piece of paper and think through your options, approaches, and plan your response.

Today's question is:

"Are you being stressed by the present, future, or do you need to make a contingency plan?"

Wednesday, January 8, 2014

365QOD- Day1068

Bulling Others

"A teacher was teaching her class about bullying and gave them the following exercise to perform. She had the children take a piece of paper and told them to crumple it up, stomp on it and really mess it up BUT be careful not to rip it.

Then she had them unfold the paper, smooth it out and look at how scarred and dirty it was. She then told them to tell it they are sorry. Now even though they said they were sorry and tried to fix the paper, she pointed out all of the scars they left behind. And that those scars will never go away no matter how hard they tried to fix it.

That is what happens when a child bullies another child, they may say they are sorry but the scars are there forever. The looks on the faces of the children in the classroom told her the message hit home."- Anonymous

I read this story as if it was written on a crumpled up piece of paper. It moved me and helped me realize the importance of our words. We have the right to say what we believe BUT that does not mean that it will not cause scarring of the other person at who the words are directed. Reality is that words can be smooth or leave scars behind that no matter how much we apologize for will never go away.

To me, it seems that we need to slow down, use a pause, and think through our words more than with do. We should not be in a rush to react and simply listen and respond a bit slower. The damage we could cause will be reduced by adding a simple pause button.

I realize that this story is about children and the words that they use and things that they do. BUT I believe that these types of actions occur in work places all of the time. Maybe the visual is enough to make us slow down and think twice before we hurt others.

Today's question is:

"Are your words leaving scars on others?"

Action

Monday, April 22, 2013

365QOD- Day807

"**Put the action step you want taken in the subject line of your email**" - Jason Womack

I watched a video today in which Jason gives this idea. In my world this advice is worth gold.

I send and receive a ton of emails each day and cannot effectively answer most of them. If I get 200 emails and choose to just open and read the emails might take anywhere from one to five minutes per email. With 100 you are looking at 100 to 500 minutes. When you have 200 then you have 200- 1000 minutes per day. There are only 480 minutes in a working day.

The idea of what action need taking would save a lot of time. This will be more and more important as more and more people read their email on mobile devices. It might result in taking more actions in a day.

Today's question is:
" **Would having an action listed in the subject line save you time reading?**"

Saturday, June 15, 2013

365QOD- Day862

"Sometimes we are forced into actions we ought to have found ourselves"- Bob Hopkins' line in Maid in Manhattan

While resting last Saturday I heard this line on TV as I was flipping channels. What a great line!

We experience life. Often we settle for what we get from others. Sometimes we even have the strength to demand what we want.

However, this line indicates that at times we are forced to do something that we should be known enough to do but have refused. We might have thought about doing something but it did not translate into action. In other words we gave ourselves an out. The actions of others forced us into action.

Today's question is:
" **Can you make** yourself **to do something without others forcing you to do it?**"

Thursday, June 20, 2013

365QOD- Day 867

"Fortes fortuna adiuvat " - Latin version of fortune favors the bold

In 2008 many people felt the economy collapsing around them. Some people choose to start businesses. Was it fear? Was it having a great idea? An Inc. magazine study reveals the reasons why people started their businesses.

In a story titled **No Time Like the Present** they report that 4 percent of founders cited job loss as reason for starting a business. This seems low but maybe being forced to do something is not big enough of a reason to start a business.

Second group, 50 percent, believed that their idea will succeed even in economic downturn. In other words the idea moved them forward toward executing it even if timing was not perfect.

Last group, 46 percent, recognized the gamble and could not resist seizing the opportunity. I would say they were afraid but did it anyway because they believed it to be worth it in the end.

After reading this story I believe that the recipe is to be bold, 96 percent, brings favors from fortune. Bold execution is everything.

Today's question is:
"Do you move boldly toward things you want?"

Sunday, January 5, 2014

365QOD- Day1065

The Five Second Rule- Tricking Yourself Into Action

"If you want to change anything about your life just do the things that you don't feel like doing."- Mel Robbins

I discovered Mel this weekend. I happen to be listening to TED talks and her speech moved me. It moved me enough to look her up and watch some of her other spots on various shows. One of the YouTube videos was for Success magazine. In it she says the above quote and other words of wisdom.

One of the things that she speaks of is anti-actions. These are actions such as surfing the web, updating Facebook, watching TV, updating twitter, etc. that fill your time and take away from your true work. I completely agree. These things are easy and require no effort. They are mindless time fillers.

She speaks of, "every time you push through you are making a long term investment in yourself". So every time we push through the 'I don't feel like it' we are building our muscles for taking actions. We have to make now the time instead of saying that this is not the time. In reality, we will never feel like it. We have to take action anyway.

I believe that the best way to build this muscle is to execute the 5 second rule:

When you get a thought to do something towards your goal to immediately start, within 5 seconds, and get momentum to move you forward.

So the only question you should quickly ask is, "Is this action strategic towards my goals or an anti-action?" If the answer is first then do not stop and start doing it.

Today's question is:
"Are you going to execute the 5 second rule?"

Balance

Wednesday, June 12, 2013

365QOD- Day859

" Be quiet, I am catching up on my ultradian rhythm"- a joke

What are ultradian rhythms? Ultradian rhythms are mini mind and body breaks that one strategically takes during the day.

Our bodies need nourishment and rest to perform properly. Without proper nutriment every 90-120 minutes they start getting hungry and the longer we go without feeding it we are more likely to overeat. So when we override the 90-120 minute natural cycle we tend to do things that we should not.

Same thing goes for or minds. If your mind does not take a mental break every 90-120 minutes it does not stay sharp. It will start making mistakes more frequently.

Putting this together would mean that every hour and a half or two hours we should grab something light to eat and rest by closing our eyes and stilling our mind.

Today's question is:
" Could you take a 10-15 minute break mentally and physically every 90 -120minutes?"

Friday, June 21, 2013

365QOD- Day868

"Too much consistency inevitably leads to a plateau where weaknesses ossify and improvement becomes harder."- Scott Young

In past posts I have written about the power of a routine. The power of routines is that they become automatic and do not require much conscious thinking to get things done.

But to grow we must stretch. We have to constantly put ourselves in situations where we disrupt our routines, push the limits to a new limit, and get out of our comfort zone. So what is the sweet spot between routine and stretching?

Scott Young in his 99U presentation offers a way of striking a balance between routine and true growth. His suggestions are:"
1. Purposely taking on projects to learn new skills.
2. Setting "deep focus" hours to consciously push your skill set forward.
3. Instead of changing your habits, changing your environment in order to force habit change and learning
"

In my world, I believe that 20 percent of our time must be spent stretching and 80 should be spent developing routines.

Today's question is:
"What is the right balance between routine and stretching for you?"

Thursday, January 16, 2014

365QOD- Day1076

Awareness of Five Minutes

"Durr, a new concept wristwatch that buzzes every five minutes, in an effort to jolt you into doing something with your day."-Jason O. Gilbert

A while back I wrote about a Mindfulness App I have been using for a while. The app randomly sounds a meditation bell once per hour from 9 am to 9 p.m. The purpose of the app is for you to stop and think about what you are doing and whether you are mindful.

Initially I used the app a lot but at times it would go off during meetings and folks would wonder what the bell sound was all about. I eventually started turning the sound off during meetings.

The idea of having a wristwatch without a working face that serves this reminder function is interesting. It provides the same reminder in five minute increments with a simple vibration. This is regular repetition teaching you physically the meaning of five minutes. Most of us are aware that when we do unpleasant tasks those five minutes seems like an hour.

I believe that initially it would be wonderful especially since you are not bothering others. BUT I believe that after a while your body would tune into the repeated vibration and you would start to ignore it.

Today's question is:

"Would you find it helpful or ignore a five minute vibration reminder?"

Belief

Tuesday, February 19, 2013

365QOD- Day745

"Impossible contains I'm possible" – Audrey Hepburn

Recently I notice this quote. I created my own version of this quote
Impossible
I'mpossible
I'm possible

What is the difference? I introduced an obvious transition piece. But it is more than that.

Notice that the transition piece puts an accent on the I. In other words I have to find it within myself in order for the transition to occur. The only way for the transition between the first and second pieces to happen is for one to sit down and understand what those beliefs are and why they are believed to be true.

Another transition has to occur is between the second piece and third pieces. Once you understand your current beliefs, you have to create the new beliefs that will make you see it as a new reality.

BUT it cannot be just mental. In other words I can tell myself that I believe all kinds of things BUT I might not act like it. In order for me to act on that new belief that something is possible I have to attach emotions to that belief. This involves repetition of the belief while 'feeling' it true. You have to get yourself 'pumped up' with that belief as if your life depends on it.

Today's question is:
"What do you believe is impossible?"

Friday, March 1, 2013

365QOD-Day755

"..awakening from an inauthentic life..." - Gloria Steinem

I listened to a CD set called **I Believe** that is based on a PBS program. It was great because it allowed people of all walks of life to tell us what they genuinely believed. They were restrained from telling the audience what they did not believe.

The line above was a part of a segment that Gloria recorded. I just loved the combination of words.

Recently I have been working on creating a table of contents for my autobiography called Un-Examined Life. Each day I go through my outline and add a few lines that will fill a page or a chapter. In a sense I am awakening in order to write this book.

The audience? Me and my children. If no one else reads it then it would be OK with me. It is a gift to give them the answers to why I made the choices throughout my life. To examine my choices and determine if they were consistent with who I am. In my opinion this is a difficult level to reach.

Today's question is:
"Are you living an authentic life?"

Wednesday, March 6, 2013

365QOD-Day760

"Productivity per hour" - a measure

I watched an old 60 minute piece about how people are working extremely long hours. It seems people are connected through laptops, email, voice mail, and cell phones to their job 24/7. Some people are working 15 hours per day connected to their job.

The French people tend to take 5 weeks of vacation per year and tend to work 300 hours less than us Americans. This statement made me wonder if we are busy or just crazy busy? Just because someone is trying to earn the 80 hours per week badge, it does not mean they are more productive than someone working 40 hours per week. It is quantity vs. quality of the time that matters.

The way one French writer explained it is that we Americans believe that the future will be better than the present and the French believe that the present will be better than the future. This is a striking difference in mindset.

I know that when I come back from vacation I feel recharged and ready to make a difference. Maybe I am unusual but I take my vacation and often combine it with my schedule to give myself time to read and introduce new ideas into my mind. Ideas I would be too busy to work on while working a full week.

Today's question is:
"What is your productivity per hour?"

Wednesday, April 3, 2013

365QOD- Day788

"Two guys quit"-a surprise announcement

Recently a company I work with lost two key employees. It was a shock to the leadership.

My question was to what their strategy is for keeping them or replacing them. Both strategies seemed reasonable.

This event made me think how replaceable any of us are to an employer. Everyone is important to a team. Some members might even argue that they are more important than others.

I tend to think in terms of all of us being links in a chain. So yes some are more important and missed longer but in the end the hole is filled by someone else.

Today's question is:
"How replaceable are you?"

Friday, April 5, 2013

365QOD- Day790

"Fasting...I hate that"- My belief

As a followers of Eastern Orthodox we tend to fast during lent. I have never been given a great reason to fast. I do not think God cares whether we do or do not fast.

But maybe I am wrong?

The other day I watched a PBS show in which a reporter showed the effects that fasting had on a person's health. The hour long show discussed the benefits of four different types of fasts.

The four types were:
1. Reduced intake,
2. Three day fast of only water, black tea, and fifty calorie soup each day,
3. One day 25 percent of normal intake followed by an eat anything day
4. Five days of normal intake followed by two day fast.

The reporter choose the five and two and lost fourteen pounds and all his health screens were incredibly great.

I personally liked the one day on, one day off. You would think that a person would stuff themselves the second day. Reality was that typically people ate only 110 percent the second day. In other words 110+25=135 or 67.5 percent of normal. This is a reduction of a little more than a third of normal intake.

This show completely changed my opinion because it clearly showed me the benefits of fasting on health.

Today's question is:
"Could you be wrong about a practice?"

Tuesday, April 9, 2013

365QOD- Day794

"If you play a good team then momentum will swing 3-5 times, with a great team it might only happen once"- paraphrase of Rick Patino

This weekend I found myself glued to the NCAA final four. It had two very good games: Louisville vs. Wichita State and Michigan vs. Syracuse.

I usually do not care who wins but I wanted Wichita to beat Louisville. They got ahead by up to 10 points but in the end they lost. Similarly, Michigan got ahead by 10 points but held on to win.

Observing this made me wonder why one team won and the other lost. Was it talent? Based on play I would say Wichita was the best of the four and should have won it all. Athletically, all four teams had gifted players.

I believe that it all boiled down to belief. Somewhere in the back of the minds of the WS player's was a belief that they did not belong in the championship game.

Interestingly, the same thing happened Monday in the final between Michigan and Louisville. Michigan came out and was smoking Louisville. There was player on Michigan's team that scored six out of six three points in the first half but scored nothing in the second half. Louisville believed and won the game.

Today's question is:
"What beliefs that you hold prevent you from reaching your next level?"

Wednesday, July 3, 2013

365QOD- Day880

"Competing commitments- this is when one of our conscious goals bumps into
one of our unconscious beliefs and it is quietly but brutally clobbered by it."-Robert Kegan

I believe that underneath us all is a very complex machine. It records evening it hears, sees, tastes, etc. Our minds are perfect recorders.

Once this data comes in, the three layers of the brain process the data. Some of the information is new and must be either accepted or rejected. This is where the quote above comes into play.

Over time we form our unconscious beliefs. They are like icebergs underneath the sea. We can see the top of the iceberg (conscious) but underneath might hide more than 80 percent of it(unconscious).

The unfortunate part for us is that the unconscious will kill off new information that does not fit with current beliefs. The only way to overcome this is to continuously expose yourself to new data, hope that over time your brain will see the benefit of this new information and start believing it.

Today's question is:
"How do you expose yourself to new data?"

Sunday, November 3, 2013

365QOD- Day1002

Belief and Action

"You are what you believe yourself to be."- Paulo Coelho

Many blogs ago I shared a quote by Henry Ford, **"If you think you can or you can't, you are right."** I love that quote because it teaches us how important is having a belief of whether we can do something or not. It teaches us that we place artificial limits on ourselves.

The quote by Paulo extends this to our belief of what we are. If we believe we are good then we must be good, if we believe that we are smart then we must be smart, etc. It is a belief.

The interesting part is to combines these two ideas into one: **We are what we believe ourselves to be and we will do what we are capable of.**

So if we want to be something different then we must start believing that we are different. That is a start but we must combine it with belief that what we want to do we are capable of doing. Paulo's quote is a prerequisite for Ford's.

Today's question is:
"What do you believe yourself to be?"

Thursday, November 21, 2013

365QOD- Day1020

Assumptions

"If I'm not getting the result I want, what are my assumptions?"- Tim Ferriss

In a past post I told a story of being stressed out about a change and asking myself a powerful question,"What is that I would have to believe for this to be true?" It immediately took me out of the mindset that I had of, "Ohhh no this is happening to me" into examining what needed to change. Once I identified the base of my belief (fear) I was able to challenge it and find a way to resolve my issue.

Tim's advice is for getting yourself to overcome a limitation. In my opinion and Tim's quote, most of the time the limitation in the result that we are getting or not getting is in the assumptions that we make. For example, if my assumption is that I cannot touch a basketball rim then my result is always going to be less than touching the rim.

The key is to stop at the result and to ask yourself to identify what are those assumptions. If I realize that that is my assumption then I might need a training program that improves my vertical jump until I comfortably reach the rim. After all if a 5 foot 3 inch former basketball star Spud Webb could reverse dunk a basketball then clearly my assumptions are holding me back.

Assumptions are not always physical but they are always mental. If I do not believe I can, then no matter how easy the task is I will not accomplish it. It is mind over matter.

Today's question is:
"Do you ever question your assumptions or do you just blindly accept them?"

Tuesday, December 3, 2013

365QOD- Day1032

What do You Truly Value

"Values do not get communicated, they get revealed"- Paul Balmert

A couple of years ago I wrote a post about a seminar I attended dealing with determining one's strengths and how to improve them. The seminar was called StrengthFinder 2.0. I loved the seminar.

One of the exercises, about which I wrote about in a post, was on determining our one true value. We started with 10 values each. We were then were asked to get rid of half of them. This was hard. But then the instructors asked us to cut it down to three. There were tears and pain at this point. Lastly, the leaders asked us to get rid of two of the last three values. In the end we were left with a singular value that was the most meaningful for us. Some of us did not like the answer but the reality was that it was the one value which ruled us above all the other ones.

Paul uttered the quote of the day during a safety leadership seminar today. By connecting the two events, immediately I saw why many companies and leaders fail. The focus is on communicating but not necessarily having the value as "the one" value. It is the difference between words vs. actions. It is hard for companies to go through the soul searching exercise that I underwent. Impossible! So they settle for words.

Today's question is:
"What is the one value you hold dear above all?"

Ben

Saturday, July 20, 2013
365QOD- Day896

"X is our company value"- usually empty words

I have worked for companies that make statements in this form about what they believe they truly value. Amazingly they value X until it costs them too much and then they change it. Some companies truly follow their values but those are rare.

One of the companies that follow their values is Southwest. Recently, while listening to an audio book I heard that every potential employee is given a personality test. They have to score at a certain level to be given employment.

The personality test that Southwest administers measures the strength of these seven values:
1. Cheerfulness
2. Optimism
3. Decision making skills
4. Communication
5. Team spirit
6. Self-starter
7. Self confidence

Most interviews that I have conducted try to establish whether the person is intrinsically or externally motivated. They never go deep into what the person values.

Today's question is:
"What personality traits does your company reward?"

Brand

Tuesday, February 12, 2013
365QOD- Day738

"I wonder what it takes to get to the 1%" - my reaction

Yesterday I got an email from LinkedIn. It said, "You have one of the top 5% most viewed LinkedIn profiles for 2012!"

Man it made me feel great. I have 500+ connections but that is nothing compared to many others. I spend maybe 1 hour per month nurturing the relationships. In other words, I have put my profile up and just done the bare minimum.

My blog posts do not even get posted on it. Imagine if I put my posts up on the site. Maybe it would drive my traffic to this blog and improve my rating? Maybe it would push me into the 1%?

So what? Well, marketing these days is mostly about social media. LinkedIn is a powerful weapon. Maybe nurturing it would help my brand and improve my marketing? It is a wakeup call to me.

Today's question is:
"What powerful weapons are you ignoring?"

Wednesday, October 2, 2013

365QOD- Day970

My Brand

"Your app is your brand now"-Peter Coffee article title

Earlier this year I published an app called **Business Academy**. It was my first app and it allowed me to figure out how to go from an idea, through design, to formatting it for publishing, to getting it published.

The title of this story caught my attention. The app that I designed was not intended to be my brand but a simple experiment. It does fit the cREATOR with a small c brand that I am trying to build for myself. So maybe the title fits me?

I mentioned in another post that before creating a new product and putting it out, I always ask myself if the product fits my brand. If it does not then I need to consider producing and publishing it under a creative name in order not to dilute my brand.

Today's question is:
"What do you stand for?"

Saturday, October 26, 2013

365QOD- Day994

Phones are the New Cars

"People used to customize their cars now they customize their phones"-Roland, a barber shop patron

I went to get my haircut today. This is a once a month event for me. I always look forward to it because it usually involves having a conversation that does not fit the mold with another customer.

Roland stated talking about cars of yesterday and how kids in the past used to modify them to fit their personalities and show uniqueness. He said that he felt that today the cell phone is what they modify.

I argued that even though I agree with him on the modifying, it does not fit the same need. When someone modifies a car they want everyone to notice them. How do I notice the app you installed that you think is cool?

In my opinion, it is only through purchasing a new phone that you get uniqueness. But anyone can go out and buy that phone and your uniqueness just disappeared.

Today's question is:
"How do you stand out as being unique?"

Monday, January 20, 2014

365QOD- Day1080

Three Types of Entrepreneurship Success Stories- Type1

"There are said to be only a handful of plot lines in all of world literature- as few as seven or as many as 20, depending on which comp-lit professor is counting. Through the cannon of business- start up tales is not exactly literature, I count at least three narratives"- Eric Schurenberg, Inc. magazine editor

According to Eric, the first type of start up story is the <u>Rags to Riches</u>. This is the story in which the start up founder takes an existing good business and drives it to greatness. From good to great is hard to do. Jim Collins details how difficult it is for good companies to become great in his classic book Good to Great.

An example of a founder that fits the Rags to Riches narrative is Sam Walton. He started a single Ben Franklin store and eventually created the giant Walmart. The great company continues to grow even years after his death. That is a perfect example of taking a good store and creating a great company.

A more recent example of this is Gary Vaynerchuk. He took his family liquor store and grew it into an online presence Wine Library TV channel. Again, he grew it from a good one store to a giant within the industry.

The reason for writing this post is to ask yourself if this type of narrative fits your life story. Does it feel natural? Is it believable? You are the only one that will know. But you will never be believable if you don't believe it.

Today's question is:
"Does your life story fit the Rags to Riches narrative?"

Tuesday, January 21, 2014
365QOD- Day1081

Three Types of Entrepreneurship Success Stories- Type2

"OK Rags to Riches does not fit me. What is the second type?"- A realization

According to Eric, the second type of start up story is the We Built It, They Came. This is the story in which the start up founder creates a product for their own need. The founder is doing this for themselves BUT almost immediately customers start to demand the product.

An example of a founder that fits the We Built It, They Came narrative is Howard Schultz. He started a single coffee shop that eventually created the giant Starbucks. The key to their success is by creating a third place away from work or home that people can meet and hang out.

A more recent example of this is Mark Zuckerberg. He took his need to communicate with his classmates friends and grew it into a Facebook. He grew it from being relevant on one campus into the giant that everyone connects through.

The reason for writing this post is to ask yourself if the We Built It, They Came narrative fits your life story? Does it feel natural? Is it believable? You are the only one that will know. But you will never be believable to others if you don't believe it.

Today's question is:
"Does your life story fit the We Built It, They Came narrative?"

Wednesday, January 22, 2014

365QOD- Day1082

Three Types of Entrepreneurship Success Stories- Type3

"OK I Built It, BUT They did not Come. What is the third type?"- A second realization

According to Eric, the third type of start up story is the We Saw a Need, We Filled It. This is the story in which the start up founder observes the need in others and creates a product for their need. The founder is doing this for others AND almost immediately customers start to demand the product.

An example of a founder that fits the We Saw a Need, We Filled It is Sara Blakely. She saw a need for a slimming product by other women and filled the need by creating Spanx.

The reason for writing this post is for you to ask yourself if the We Saw a Need, We Filled It narrative fits your life story. Does it feel natural? Is it believable? You are the only one that will know. But you will never be believable to others if you don't believe it.

Today's question is:
"Does your life story fit the We Saw a Need, We Filled It narrative?"

Business

Wednesday, February 20, 2013

365QOD- Day746

"Analog vs. anti-log" – new idea

While reading Lean Startup book by Ries I came across his explanation of the concepts of analog and anti-log.

Often times, when in the process of creating we can see how something is an extension on to something that already exists. In the book the author gives the analog example of creating a iPod device like the Sony Walkmen. It was just an upgrade to existing device that people were using. The Walkmen showed that people were willing to listen to music in public with little earphones in the ears.

So what is an anti-log? Consider the time frame during which the iPod was created. Napster was king and allowing people to illegally download music. This was an indication that people would download music BUT also that they were not willing to pay for it. Napster was the anti-log.

Combining those two concepts gives you the iTunes store where music can be downloaded easily and a person pays for a single song.

Today's question is:
"What are the analog and anti-log concepts related to your idea?"

Friday, February 8, 2013

365QOD- Day734

"Do you want fries with that" – A McDonalds question

I do not know if it is still true today but many years ago McDonald's employees were trained that after a person placed an order to ask if the person wants fries with that. Why? Because McDonald's recognizes that the markup on fries is incredible.

Think about it like this. A good deal 10 lbs. of potatoes are usually about $3. In it you probably get 20 potatoes. So if you take 2 of those and convert them into fries that you sell for a minimum of $1 then you just converted $3 into $10. So McDonald's knows what is the most profitable item and by selling more of it they maximize their profits. (I happen to think their McDouble is a great deal for $1 but their fries are not such a great deal)

The moral of that story is that you need people to buy into your ideas and you need to know which ideas give you the biggest bang for your buck.

Today's question is:
"What is the most profitable thing you sell?"

Friday, February 22, 2013

365QOD- Day748

"Four key questions
1. Do customers recognize that they have the problem you are trying to solve?
2. If there was a solution, would they buy it?
3. Would they buy it from us?
4. Can we build a solution for that problem?" –Lean Startup by Al Ries

While reading the book Lean Startup by Al Ries I came across these four questions. Recently I have been working on learning how to develop apps that would teach math concepts that students did not learn well in high school. I would like to be able to create apps that teach a little theory, show a few examples, and provide a tool to continue the learning. So how would I answer these questions?

Q1 answer: There is a large group of students going into I believe that most students are using their smart phones in innovative ways. If a tool is given to them to learn a concept then they will test it. If the tool can effectively teach them the concept then they will embrace it.

Q2 answer: When I did a search on apps that provide a tool for learning math there did not exist one as interactive as mine. I believe as long as I provide 4 lessons per app for $1 they will buy it.

Q3 answer: Since my apps are the only ones that provide the tool, then there is no competition. If they are going to buy an app that teaches them 4 lessons per app then they will buy mine.

Q4 answer: I have build the solution to the math problem and presented it to a major on-line university several years ago. They chose not to buy from me but created their own versions.

Today's question is:
"Do you have an idea to put through the four questions?"

Monday, February 25, 2013

365QOD- Day751

"A cool story"- My review

I watched the movie The Words last weekend. It was a very good movie. It was three stories within one. It was a story of a reader and his life. He was reading a story of a man who found and published a book by a third man. Last story was of the third guy. It was interesting story because it made you a part of three different lives and how they connected. The connection was the reader.

Lately I have been wondering if people are interested in reading great stories. I mean a short story that pulls you in and never lets you go. Recently, I read several Leo Tolstoy short stories and I can tell you that there is power behind a short story.

The entrepreneur side of me immediately wondered if a short story is worth 99 cents. Just like an app? Would people pay for a great short story? Maybe they already are? I am ignorant about the market.

I do believe that a great short story is no different than a great website, great blog, great book, etc. Without people being exposed to it, it dies a quiet death. Without social media it is very difficult and costly to get anyone's attention.

Today's question is:
"Which one of your products is dying a quiet death?"

Monday, March 4, 2013

365QOD-Day758

"So what should I charge?"- Tommy's question

Tommy is a connector. He knows a lot of people and is in a position where he can offer a connection to someone looking to grow their business. Tommy knows people who know people.

The other day we had a conversation and he wondered out loud what his services were worth. It was an excellent question. Compensation for an introduction would be different than compensation for future business.

After some thought I came up with:
fees= IntroductionFee + Percent*(FutureBusiness)

The introduction fee should be small enough to not feel like a demand but a reward. The way I see it that the one person you are connecting is looking to expand their business and should be willing to reward you for the introduction. A good number? $500 is an acceptable fee in my mind.

The future business is the potential business that could result from the introduction. This number as well as the Percent that are acceptable create the biggest challenge. If the business will earn 1M new business then 2% is not unreasonable.

Putting it together for a situation where an introduction would lead to 1M on new business is:
**fee=500+.02*1000000
fee=500+20000
fee=20500**

If they meet but do not end up doing business then $500 is the fee. If they do more than 1M then the Percent*FutureBusiness portion grows.

Today's question is:
"How valuable are your connections?"

Saturday, April 8, 2013

365QOD- Day791

"How can they stay in business?"- My thought

I am reading a book called **Laptop Millionaire**. It is in an eBook format. Easy to read but I decided that I want to purchase it in order to work with it.

I looked on Amazon and it was 13 plus shipping. Abebooks had it for 8 plus shipping. When I called BN in Houston they told me that they have it in stock and that it is 22 but 13 online.
I immediately thought that there is no way Barnes and Noble can continue operating that way.

I love bookstores. I can easily spend hours in bookstores looking through books and generating new ideas. In a post before I even cried about Boarders on Michigan Avenue in Chicago closing. It broke my heart.

The bookstore business must be a very tough business. But when the discrepancy between online and brick and mortar store is so great then people will choose online. Unfortunately online does not fill my other need of browsing the same way.

Bookstores, like coffee places, are places, like home and office, where one can spend time talking with people about ideas. They feel like a nurturing space. However, I am not convinced that their future is very bright.

Today's question is:
"What will be the next third place where people can just hang out?"

Wednesday, April 24, 2013

365QOD- Day809

"Most businesses fail because owners work in their business instead of on their business"- Michael Gerber

I was listening to an audio book today and the author of Emyth stated a version of this quote. I immediately agreed with him.

I have been around many CEOs and many do not have businesses that they can sell. They have no systems. They just show up for work and without them the business slows down or stops.

If you do not have training manuals for each position and training for new people in each role then you are not running a true business. You are running lean and if any one decides to quit then you will feel immense pain. The more systems you have the easier it is for you to convince an outsider that you are not needed for day to day operations and the business could be bought if profitable.

Today's question is:
"Do you believe in systems or are you just in business?"

Friday, May 24, 2013

365QOD- Day840

"Regardless of the city you're in, you get into your car and your preferences climate control, radio and seat positioning settings, itinerary destination, even favorite restaurants are already programmed in"- Luke Schneider

This morning I read a story about a new rental car company called Silvercar. What caught my attention is that it only uses silver Audi cars and the based on the quote the car becomes customizable.

My first thought was that there isn't enough of a demand but maybe I am wrong. Maybe we all want things to be customized to us? It seems that our attitude is "it is all about me".

I can imagine that getting in a car that feels like yours could be wonderful. But sometimes the fun is in playing with the gadgets and the different settings. It is fun until you get it just perfect for you. I hate it when I let my wife drive my car and I have to make the adjustments. This teaches me that once it is perfect for me I do not want it changed.

Today's question is:
" How customizable do things need to be for you to be useful?"

Monday, June 10, 2013

365QOD- Day857

"How may I help my customer?"-a great question

While looking through Success magazine in a bookstore I read through the ads for new books. One of the books was called Youtility by Jay Baer.

In order to stand out and to create brand loyalty, the book suggests asking yourself questions in order to determine if you are:"

1. **Giving your customers useful information through your website**
2. **Respond quickly to questions and concerns posted on social media**
3. **Offer suggestions that are helpful to your existing and potential audiences"**

For me I believe that this blog gives useful information. So I would give myself a high mark. Maybe an 8 out of 10.

I usually do not give timely response to comments. I intend the posts to make you think for yourself and not open the door for arguing the validity of my opinion. So maybe a 3. (I answer text messages)

The questions are my suggestions for stirring additional thinking to take place. I believe that I do a good job. Maybe an 8.

Overall, I give myself 19 out of possible 30. This is not an impressive score. I immediately know what I can do better to improve my brand's helpfulness score.

Today's question is:
" How do you help your customers?"

Monday, July 22, 2013
365QOD- Day898

"What is the level above customer service?"- My question to my friend

Friday night my friend Naren and I went to get some dinner. On our way to dinner we discussed customer service.

We made some observations about people around us that provide great customer service. There were a few that stood out amongst those.

This is why I asked the question above. The answer is customer recognition. Customer service occurs after the customer has started the engagement. It is the quality of that interaction that determines the quality of the customer service.

Customer recognition is a completely different game. We both have a friend that is exceptional in customer recognition. He is so good at the game that he remembers people that he has meet years ago by name. He greats them warmly by name and makes them feel welcome.

So we were having this conversation as we walked into the restaurant. Out server April immediately recognized us, noted the missing member of our trio, and asked why we had not been there in three weeks. Impressive! In a sentence she made us feel welcome and missed. We told her our conversation topic. She said thanks for recognizing it.

Today's question is:
"How good is your customer recognition?"

Wednesday, August 14, 2013

365QOD- Day921

Timeless Advice

"Adapt what is useful, reject what is useless, and add what is specifically your own."-Bruce Lee

While flipping through a Men's Health magazine I came across this quote. Although at first it seems to be specific to fitness, it is very applicable to many areas. Let me tell you a story.

I am currently sitting in a PMP (Project Management Professional) study course. Its focus is on passing the exam but amazingly my coworkers and I are learning a lot about general project management theory. So seeing the whole is helping us connect it to what we do.

Our internal project management process is but a subset of the whole. So while in class we have had discussions as to what we believe is useful to us in our improvement efforts. We can clearly see how some of the topics would be useful to add to our flow.

Just as easy it is to see what is useless. The process is detailed that for some of the work that we do it is overkill. We would be wasting time and money implementing it all. Therefore we have to be strategic in determining what is useless as much as figuring out what is helpful.

The last part of quote is very insightful. If says no matter what the system is you can benefit by adding something that is uniquely yours. A great example of this is cooking a meal. You have things you add and things you do not add because they do not improve the meal. But the magic occurs when you add the seasonings. Everyone flavors it differently and in differing amounts. That adds the POW!

Today's question is:
"What is useful, useless, and your addition to your process?"

Wednesday, November 6, 2013

365QOD- Day1005

More Expensive than Gold

"The processed venom can fetch as much as $7000 per ounce"- Men's Journal article on venom collecting

The other morning I was reading a story about a man who nurtures 280 diamondback rattlesnakes. Every two weeks he milks his 280 snakes and each one gives him 3/4 of a gram of venom. In other words the 280 snakes give him a total of 210 grams of venom. Since there are 28 grams per ounce this results in 7.5 ounces. In other words $7000*7.5= $52,500 every two weeks.

Wow! This is a serious business since the venom is used by pharmaceutical companies to make medications.

I do not like snakes but this is an impressive business. At over a million, the person running it is earning over a million. His costs would be feeding the snakes two mice per month which is about $1 and the healthy maintenance of these animals. In other words minimal cost high maintenance.

So why do I care? Most of us would not believe the profitability of this dangerous business. Yes it is dangerous BUT once you master the handling of these snakes the rest is pure business. It is scary to those of us who do not like to handle snakes but I believe a viable business for many who are not so squeamish.

Today's question is:
"Could you handle running a snake venom business if it means $1 million dollar per year profit?"

Monday, November 11, 2013

365QOD- Day1010

Passion Retirement

"I refuse to be old, I don't mind aging, but I will never be old."- Dwan Smith-Fortier

Most people do not live very long after they retire. Unless they have a physical goal and a mental goal, they wither and die. This is because their social network typically consists of co-workers and their mental stretches are only due to the type of work that they perform.

Recently while reading Oct 29th 2013 USA Today I came across a story about a different type of colonies that let seniors color outside lines. It was built on the idea of people there becoming involved in different types of art and creativity projects. Some got involved in an acting course, photography, some in painting courses, Zumba, etc.

About a year ago I read a book about thriving in retirement. It seems that people that do well in retirement, according to the book, are people who go back to their passions before life got in the way and explore them. This community idea seems like a perfect match for that passion pursuit.

The idea of having a retirement community built around a particular passion is wonderful. I believe it will extend most people's lives because it will give them a reason to get up in the morning. This is one of the four requirements to living to an age of 100.

Today's question is:

"If you were to retire today, what type of community would help fulfill your passion?"

Change

Monday, November 4, 2013

365QOD- Day1003

A Wasted Experience

"Waterfall, river, and lake"- the authors visualization of the ten days of meditation

This morning I was reading Men's Journal and came across an article about a guy who spent ten days in an ashram in India. It caught my interest because I felt I could learn from author's spiritual journey.

What I learned was how uncomfortable he was and how he tried to break the rules. In the end he says that he is a changed person. This did not seem real to me.

He chooses to go there to be changed, to learn how to meditate, and get closer to the source. Instead of choosing to embrace the experience he fought it and then claimed that it changed him. Maybe I am judging him?

I just feel sorry for him that he wasted such an opportunity. How many of us would have an opportunity to spend ten days learning to pray and getting closer to God? Probably not many of us.

Today's question is:
"Do you embrace the change that you want to happen or do you fight it?"

Communication

Friday, February 15, 2013

365QOD- Day741

"Everything that needs to be said has already been said. But, since no one was listening, everything must be said again."- Angre' Gide

I often worry that a post I am currently writing is one I have already written but can't remember that I wrote it. With 741 posts in my blog I cannot keep track of them in my mind any more.

I am certain that often I repeat the message but maybe in a slightly different format. Maybe it is middle age? Another way to say this is that I am re-enforcing the message.

I do believe that I do get inspired by same ideas and have to be on guard to expose myself to new thoughts and ideas. Only with new thoughts and ideas can I replace the old worn out connections in my brain.

Today's question is:
"How do you know what you have already said?"

Sunday, February 10, 2013

365QOD- Day736

"The 80/20 rule again"- My thought

I listened to two very talkative people have a conversation. I was wore out.
During the conversation one of the people kept talking and talking. Usually their typical conversations are dominated by one or the other.

So the usual format is one will start it and the other will dominate it. It works for them but I feel that it is limiting.

When I have conversations with people I want to engage with them. Maybe share something and then listen to their response and ideas. It seems to me that the 80/20 rule fits well.

I want to do the 20% and let the other person fill in the 80%. I know what I know BUT I do not know what they know. Then I expect the other person to do the 20% and for me to give them the 80% in order for me to contribute. It is also very important to be able to truly listen and absorb **(4 times as important)** what is being given to you. Unfortunately, we most often are just simply formulating our response.

Most conversations do not follow this ideal. The closer the conversations are to that ideal the more ideas we would exchange.

Today's question is:
"Can you hold an 80/20 conversation?"

Monday, March 11, 2013

365QOD- Day765

"The British are coming" - Paul Revere's warning

I recently saw an ad. It is Paul Revere, a legendary figure, as a person making a cell phone call to warn the other towns that the British are coming.

I stopped to think about this. What if phones had existed back then? What if Paul Revere had called instead of riding through the night? Would people have prepared to meet the British head on?

I believe the answer is no. If something is easy to do then it is easy not to do. The call would not have moved people as a face to face interaction between Paul and the other villagers.

Today's question is:
"Does technology make connecting on a personal level harder?"

Saturday, April 27, 2013

365QOD- Day812

"Build it, they will remain" - bad networking advice

I have been thinking about network building lately. There are people that constantly meet new people as a part of their job.

As an example, consider real estate agents. They tend to specialize in an area of a city and get to meet people looking for a place in that area. The looking process might expose them to the same people several times. Enough to potentially build a friendship.

So what?

Just because you build a network of good people it does not mean that it is very strong. If you sell these folks a house you have a temporarily gain but might never turn that into a future gain.

I believe that the network has to be nurtured once it had been created. To do this a person would have to periodically maintain contact with the network by carrying enough to call and inquire about people's lives outside of the work relationship. In my opinion 10 percent of one's time needs to be spent on nurturing.

Today's question is:
"How do you nurture your network?"

Friday, August 16, 2013

365QOD- Day923

Did you get that?

"When a message is sent up from the lowest levels to senior management, the noise level doubles and the meaning of the message is cut in half as it passes through each level in the organization's corporate hierarchy"-Peter Drucker

Communication is difficult. A message needs to be created in the sender's mind, then translated into words that we feel the other person will understand.

On the receiving end the person takes what they heard, recreates the message, and then translates it into words that they understood. Lastly, feedback is send back to the sender of what was understood.

Team communication stays at the same level so hopefully not much gets missed. But as the quote suggests a lot gets lost as the message moves up to the next level. So my boss only gets half of my message. My boss' boss gets half of that or one fourth of what I sent. Quickly the meaning changes and the intent can be used against the originator.

So what is the answer? Stop sending information up? No. Have the means for the boss and their boss to have access to the same information so that they can review it for themselves. Of course that takes time but if the decision is critical then the extra effort is worth it.

Today's question is:
"How do you know that your message got through to your leaders?"

Tuesday, August 20, 2013

365QOD- Day927

I'm Talking Here

"You cannot not communicate" -Michael Bernoff **persuasion** CD

I just started listening to a CD program whose name escapes me. The quote is from the author. It made me stop and think about it. The double negative makes it sound different. But when you re-read it, it makes perfect sense.

What we say is the smallest part of communicating. Our body and tonality make up to 93 percent of the message. So as the quote advises you that you cannot not communicate. Even if you say nothing, you are still communicating.

If we are wise, we realize this fact and decide to control the message instead of it being misconstrued by our body posture. I believe we have to adapt a confident posture and voice in order for us to be perceived as better communicators. Once we can control the body and tonality, we can focus on the last seven percent. This can be simply done by speaking a little slower.

Today's question is:
"Are you not not communicating with your posture and tonality?"

Wednesday, September 18, 2013

365QOD- Day956

Just Open It

"The cold reality is that not every email you send is opened. The average open rate is around 20 percent across all industries. That percentage doesn't really tell the complete story either. Unless you really dig into your metrics, it's unclear which 20 percent is opening your emails. It's also likely it's not the same 20 percent opening your emails every time." - Entrepreneur magazine story

I believe that most of us, between several personal and work email accounts, we all receive anywhere from hundred to two hundred emails per day. I believe this statistic is true.

Recently I wrote a post in which I recommended that the subject line should be used more effectively by making it an action subject line. Instead of saying x tell the reader what you want done with x.

For example, instead of asking for approval and using the subject line funding request for x, use please read and approve funding request for x. The reader knows what you expect: to read and to approve. Your chances of the email being read are higher and you getting the approval is higher than 20%.

Today's question is:
"How do you effectively get your emails read?"

Thursday, September 19, 2013

365QOD- Day957

Using email to sell

"Email is not a way to sell electronically; it's a way to start and have a conversation."-Gefferey James Inc. magazine story How To Sell via Email

In post Day956 I mentioned a statistic that only 20% of emails are read. Today I happen to read a story that takes about how ineffectively people use email to sell. If the response rate is 10% of the 20% then we are talking to only 2% of the target audience.

The quote provides a solution. It is all about initiating a conversation. Initiate a conversation and if the other person is interested they will respond. As an example the author offers this advice for a good conversation starter:
"prospects name, my company, company name, has a track record helping executives reduce overhead costs and increase cash flow. We recently worked with, a company known to prospect, and were able to reduce their cost by 20%.

If this interests you, I can send you a case study or detailed description of what we do for our clients.

Your contract information"

If the person reads it they should get the feeling as if they are getting something for nothing.

Today's question is:
"How would you start a conversation through email?"

Thursday, September 26, 2013

365QOD- Day964

Do Change

"I sincerely believe that behavior change is identity/belief change"- Buster Benson

Recently a young person I know started smoking. I was so disappointed. Unfortunately, overseas kids do not get the same anti-smoking propaganda. So their chances of starting and staying a smoker are greater.

So why did he choose to start? Reviewing the situation around him it was a simple case of bad peer pressure. He kept seeing his friends smoking and eventually he decided to follow. Amazing enough was that most of these peers are younger by a year.

He now identifies himself as a smoker. He does not have to say it out loud. Puffing away says it all. His identity had been changed.

So what are his choices? He can continue and let the monkey get a better grip on him or change his friends. Which one will he choose? As the quote advises, the identity that he best identifies with will control his behavior.

Today's question is:
"Can you reverse an identity change?"

Friday, October 4, 2013

365QOD- Day972

Start or Stop Talking

"When you approach two people talking, you will be acknowledged in one of two ways. If the feet of their torsos stay in place and they twist only their upper torsos in your direction, they don't really want you to join the conversation. But if their feet move to include you then you know that you are truly invited to participate."-Carol Kinsley Goman

I saw this line on the Behance web page and immediately recognized the feelings. There have been times when I felt uncomfortable stepping into a situation between two people. And there have been times when I got smiles and was warmly welcomed.

I believe that the secret is your smile. If you approach the situation with a great attitude then you are most likely will be welcomed. If internally you are judging yourself not worthy of being there then your vibe will keep you out.

The author adds that this is also true for when conversations are over. A coworker who seems to be paying attention with their upper body angled toward you but their legs and feet are towards the door, is signaling that the conversation is over.

So start paying attention to people's upper body and use body positioning as a way of telling how people feel.

Today's question is:
"How do you know that you are welcomed or done with?"

Wednesday, October 16, 2013

365QOD- Day984

Six Minutes Forty Seconds

"How bad can it be to listen to someone for six minutes and forty seconds?" -my question

This morning before I got my day started I read a couple of stories in Inc. magazine. They approached public presentations from two completely opposite angles. What helped me note this was that they were right next to each other but they did not reference each other.

The Pacha-Kucha presentation format consists of forcing yourself to having only 20 slides with each one lasting 20 seconds. So in 6:40 (six minutes and forty seconds) you are done talking. You stop. This forces the presenter to cut their slides down and to cut to the chase quickly. I can see this turning into just the facts not a lot of fluff presentation.

Second story talked about Moth storytelling. In this format you personalize the story to pull the listener in. So this format is more about taking your time and connecting to the audience.

In other words dry facts vs. touchy moving speeches. So which one is the right format? Both are ways but you need to determine what your audience needs.

I do feel that we all need to train ourselves on being able to do the 6:40. This will teach us to focus. But then go out and also learn how to tell that great story that hooks the audience. So as I said, both are correct.

Today's question is:
"Can you give a great speech in 6:40?"

Tuesday, October 29, 2013

365QOD- Day997

My Name is

"HELLO, my name is Scott"-Scott Ginsberg's introduction

Imagine walking around with a paper name tag. Unless you are in a large meeting, most likely a few people will stop you and tell you that you have a nametag on with the expectation that you remove it. But what if you want it there by design?

Scott had been doing just that for a few years. This was a strategic move to make him more approachable. It helped him land a book deal.

This old story from Success magazine made me think about how approachable we are. By design, I always have my desk in such a way as not to place a barrier between myself and the person entering my office. To me, this is critical in being approachable. People want you see you as approachable before they approach you. So why create walls?

In my opinion most people are not aware that they are building walls and that translates into being perceived as not approachable. If you want to be approachable, tear down the walls. Be the first to extend your hand. Smile first and say hello. And wear a name tag.

Today's question is:
"How approachable are you?"

Saturday, November 2, 2013

365QOD- Day1001

Out of Curiosity

"Just out of curiosity, what do you like best about your job?"- Geoffrey James

I could not sleep this morning so I started reading articles on Inc. on line. An article about asking yourself a great question came up.

The question above is a great conversation starter. It allows the other person to talk about positive aspects of their job. The opposite could be achieved if you ask about what they hate about their job.

What made me focus on this article is its focus on asking this great question of yourself. I do believe that it will lift your mood and remind you why you like your job. But to me that is limiting.

Most people self-identify with a job title. I do not. As I have written before, I identify with the word cREATOR with a small c. That word could fit whether I am working as an engineer, manager, blogger, writer, teacher, etc.

I do believe that this is a great question to ask yourself but ask it of different aspects and people that make up your life. Do not limit its power to just work or encouraging others. Ask it of your relationships, interests, friends, things and if possible let people know why you like what you like.

Today's question is:
"Just out of curiosity, what do you like about your life?"

Day 1148 out of 21000(Refer to post 12 for the meaning)

Monday, January 27, 2014
365QOD- Day1087

Your Message

"Turn your mess into a message"- speaker's advice

The other day I watched a presentation during which the speaker uttered these words. I loved the urging so much that I wrote it down. Today, I decided to write a post about it.

I believe that this quote is very relevant to me. I often write about topics of interest to me and sometimes share my growing pains. But I have never used the words 'mess' to describe my pains.

I do believe that all of us have messes. Some we share and others we try to hide. But what makes us real to others is when we do share them. This allows us to make a genuine connection to others by exposing our mess to sell the message that we are trying to pass on.

But be careful! The message has to be real in order to connect and not appear as an attempt to sell. In my opinion it has to provide a solution to the mess that people have in common with you. That is your message for getting them out of the same mess.

Today's question is:

"What are your mess and your message?"

Connections

Monday, February 4, 2013

365QOD- Day730

THANKS for two years' worth of support...
THANKS for over 1000 views in a month
THANKS for over 10000 views total
THANKS THANKS THANKS...

"I can't see that"- a lack of vision

I happen to have a boss who is a great visionary person. He can see what is wrong and what he wants instead. He is very clear of his vision.

I am an execution guy. Once he sets the vision, I have to be able to execute it by making sure all of the pieces are there and in the right place. Obstacles in front need to be identified and overcome before they become difficulties.

The two skills are complementary and not exclusive. Some people excel in one and not the other. Developing both makes you more complete as a person because most likely you will have to work alongside a vision or an execution guy.

Today's question is:
'Do you compliment your fuzzy vision with clear execution?"

Tuesday, February 5, 2013

365QOD- Day731

"Only the paranoid survive" – Andy Grove's book title

Many years ago I gave speech at a major university to an incoming freshmen engineering class. In the speech I described my world as a professor and an engineering manager in steel industry.

During the speech I told a story of how major steel got its lunch taken by mini mills because they were not paying attention to the low-end producers. In the story I told how Andy Grove went to a conference where he heard this story and he restructured the strategy at Intel to handle this threat.

As the title of his book suggests, he believes that being paranoid is helpful to survival. BUT I believe that you still have to be a bit more confident. Paranoid Confidence as Derek Flanzraich from Greatist terms it.
"I believe the best entrepreneurs develop a healthy balance of paranoia and confidence. They're vigilant and realistic while, at the same time, never lacking the gumption to believe their vision is right."

Today's question is:
"Do you exhibit Paranoid Confidence?"

Tuesday, March 12, 2013

365QOD- Day766

"They were connectors" - my answer

I wrote a post about Paul Revere yesterday. I provided my hypothesis that the effect of making communication easier also makes it more difficult to connect to people.

You probably have your doubts about this idea. Well let me give you a couple of examples.

Paul Revere was not the only rider that night. Do you know the second one? I do not know the name but I know that I have read that there were two. So why do we know Paul and not the other one?

He was a connector. Paul was a member of many clubs and groups and had a public reputation. The other person did not have the same level of influence.

Another example is Rosa Parks. She was not the first person to protest moving to the back of the bus BUT she is the one that we all remember. Why? Like Paul, Rosa was a community connector. She not only was a part of the black organizations in her town but interacted with many white people. She served as a personal tailor to many young white women getting ready for their cotillions.

Her influence was great because she belonged to many groups of different types of people. This is the same reason why Paul Revere is known today. Both Paul and Rosa connected to lots of people. They not only connected BUT connected strongly to lots of people.

Today's question is:
"How good of a connector are you?"

Friday, January 10, 2014

365QOD- Day1070

Knowledge vs. Experience

"What is the difference between knowledge and experience?"- A naïve question

Many years ago during a panel interview I was asked why I was so comfortable. I proceeded to draw on a white board my knowledge areas. These by themselves were many.

I explained to the panel that I could easily work in any one of the fields and feel comfortable. They nodded BUT what shocked them was when I showed connections between the fields, the dots, that I claimed knowledge in.

In my opinion, that is the difference between knowledge and experience. The ability to connect the knowledge pieces into a meaningful whole is where the magic occurs. Just learning and creating the dots is not enough. It is the application, after the facts are connected, that provides the strength that leads to experience.

By the way, I got the job because of that explanation.

Today's question is:

"How do you connect your dots?"

Creativity

Saturday, March 9, 2013

365QOD-Day763

"A floating mug" - an idea by Tigere Chriiga

I recently saw a picture of this mug. It was unusual.

What made it unusual is that the handle did not just simply protrude on its side. The handle was larger than normal and it ended in a little circular base with a gap of half an inch between the mug and the base.

The mug simply floats above the base. It is a piece of art that I cannot stop looking at. The cup was artsy but yet very functional because now your hand can hold the cup without squeezing your finger in the handle. In addition, hot cup will not leave a stain on your desk because of the small base.

Today's question is:
"What is the last piece of functional art that you have used?"

Sunday, March 10, 2013

365QOD- Day764

"I got an app for that!" - Something that I always wanted to say

I am no longer a "want to be" app creator. I have created an app. It is available through the Google Play store. Do a search under Business Academy. Select the apps folder. Scroll down until you find it with my name next to it.

Cool!

It feels great when the world opens up. A couple of years ago I stared writing my blog. It fills me up every day. It lead to me finishing my first book. After I finished my first book I could not believe it why I had not done that before. This lead to me writing my second book.

Now I have started creating apps. I plan to create a new app every month. This might seem optimistic BUT it is not. Recently, I created a "shell" which will allow me to just insert screen shots into in order to get my ideas to be implemented quickly. It is in a sense a jig that will provide consistence and ease to create the apps.

I am going to focus on creating apps this year. I have even placed a slogan on my wall "The Year of the Apps...". NEXT year will be the year of the video. My creative universe is growing.

Today's question is:
"Do you know your NEXT?"

Thursday, March 14, 2013

365QOD- Day768

"Wow.. cool picture"- My typical observation

As an engineer I am not supposed to appreciate art like I do. But man when I see a picture that moves me it is no different than words or music that move me.

Maybe I allow myself? I am always taking pictures of pictures. I probably have over 1000 such pictures that I have taken in the last few years.

My newest addiction is Facebook pictures with slogans. I can't seem to get enough. I read them and appreciate the picture. If they truly move me I download it.

Sometimes I even create a slide show to reemphasize them.

Today's question is:
"What moves you enough to stop and notice?"

Saturday, April 20, 2013

365QOD- Day 805

"Making the simple complicated is commonplace; making the complicated simple, really simple, that is creativity" - Charles Mingus

While looking through a book called **Red Thread Thinking** I spotted this little gem. It immediately resonated with me.

For the last year I have been working on a product. The product could potentially result in a mass appeal product.

Well having a billion dollar idea means nothing until you execute it elegantly. Most of my solutions have been good but not simple.

The quote educated me that maybe I was stuck in a box. I needed to jump out of the box and stretch my creativity. This creativity stretch resulted in making the product simpler.

Today's question is:
"Do you always choose simplicity?"

Tuesday, April 30, 2013

365QOD-Day815

"Be curious" - Ernest Chan

This morning our class discussed a technique for establishing relationships between several inputs and a single output. It was interesting.

Besides bring interesting, it was also somewhat trial and error. You had to follow the
P-consider practical
G-graph relationships
A-analyze the data
technique.

But more than a single technique, you had to remain open and curious to the underlying relationships. Without being open you will not find the relationship between variables.

Today's question is:
"**How do you stay curious?**"

Wednesday, May 22, 2013
365QOD- Day838

"Gloria Price, professor at UC Irvine, found that technology workers got interrupted on the average every 11 minutes then it took 25 minutes to get back on track." - Source unknown

Recently I read an article that talked about two different types of schedules: a creative's and a manager's. It immediately made me think about my schedule and that of the people around me.

I am on a manager schedule. If there is an empty spot on it, schedule a meeting, and I will be there. This type of schedule trends to work in one hour blocks.

The independent contributors, the creative workers, tend to work in blocks of time bigger than an hour. So stopping in and asking a question throws them of their flow. As the quote above suggests, they lose their place and have a hard time getting back on track. The non-creative types need to give them freedom from interruption during those blocks.

Even though I follow the manager type of schedule I probably need to block out twenty percent of my time (two four hour blocks for creative work). This will allow me to create and respond to requests instead of rushing to another meeting.

Today's question is:
" What type of schedule do you follow?"

Friday, June 14, 2013

365QOD- Day861

"Overnight sensation" - an oxymoron

When I read a story about an overnight sensation I am doubtful that it is true. This was the case the other day.

I noticed a story about a mathematician who published a solution to a difficult problem dealing with prime numbers that many great mathematicians failed to solve.

Dr. Zhang graduated with a doctorate but failed to get an academic position. He worked as an accountant and in a Subway. His life does not follow in a traditional path of a great mathematician.

The article also said something else that made me think. It claimed that when one examines his work it is not that he was inspired and that it had a spark of greatness. The article claimed that his work showed great persistence in applying existing methods that other mathematicians failed to apply. In other words he outworked them while they waited to be inspired.

It is a great story that illustrates that sometimes we might just need to persevere through our work instead of looking for a spark of genius.

Today's question is:
"Can you outwork most of your coworkers?"

Saturday, August 31, 2013

365QOD- Day938

How does it feel to hold it?

"There is nothing like the feeling of seeing your child for the first time."- My words

I remember the birth of my two children, Stefani and Milan, as if it was yesterday. Both births were special and both came early in the morning. Then the hard part of parenting begins.

The other day when my third book got published I felt like I had given birth to another child. Now the parenting begins. If no one knows the book exists then does it truly matter that it was written?

Right after my third book was published I revised my ETF book and got a proof copy to review and correct. My fourth book arrived yesterday and I could not but glow as a new parent. But again, the hard parts of editing, publishing, and nurturing are not done.

Today's question is:
"Do you nurture your products or just sell them?"

Friday, September 20, 2013
365QOD- Day958

Sparks

" Expressed in plain English, this means that a single moment of insight is the result of thinking that happens before it--often, the authors state, due to reorganizing or restructuring the elements of a situation or problem. This echoes the favored Fast Company definition of creativity, that it's finding the connections between seemingly unrelated things."- Drake Barr in Fast Company article Creativity is Just Persistence, and Science Can Prove it

According to John Kounios of Drexel University and Mark Beeman of Northwestern University, "although the experience of insight is sudden and can seem disconnected from the immediately preceding thought, these studies show that insight is the culmination of a series of brain states and processes operating at different time scales."

The words series of brain states caught my interest. This holds true for me. I usually have to be thinking about something for a while before I get to the aha moment. So in a sense when I am thinking about a topic I am moving from one state to another until I get to the creative state.

Now notice the second portion of the quote, "at different time scales". In other words, these states can be close or far apart in terms of time. If we spend more time thinking about something then the states seem close to one another. So the spark does not seem so big but if the states are somewhat apart then the jump seemed big enough to be defined as an aha moment.

These two pieces together tell us that by being persistent to work on something for a while we will get to the creative state. The only unknown is time.

Today's question is:
"Do you know how to be persistent to move though different brain states quickly?"

Sunday, December 8, 2013

365QOD- Day1037

How to Tell Stories- Level1

"Tell me a story about myself when I was young"- My daughter's typical urging

The other day I was flipping through a bunch of books. One of them was a book called <u>Epic Content Marketing</u> by Joe Pulizzi. In the book I saw a figure that tried to explain story telling as having three levels. Immediately it made me think of my blog. I will try to illustrate it by using my blog as an example in this and next two posts.

The first level in blog storytelling is **Content Awareness**.

When starting to tell stories to an unknown audience the first requirement for Content Awareness is **Trust(T)**. You have to create the trust necessary for people to believe what you are telling them is the truth. As you know, it is very hard to build trust over time with people and extremely easy to lose it in a moment or post. So write what you believe and be truthful.

Second requirement is to **Be Found(BF)**. So what if you are creating very good trustworthy **content if no one can find you?** You have to be able to pull new visitors continuously in order for you to want to continue telling your stories. If you are a blog leader with no followers, you are simply wasting time writing. At every opportunity tell people about your blog and invite them to come and check it out.

I believe that over time you will reach the third requirement: **Generate Greatness(GG)**. I can definitely tell you that I am still not happy with my writing level. I know I can write much much better if I spent more time planning, writing, and editing. My compromise to me is to write daily with passion and do the editing at the end of the year when I put the book together.

Reducing this to an equation:
$$CA = T + BF + GG$$

Today's question is:
"How do you generate awareness of your content?"

Monday, December 9, 2013

365QOD- Day1038

How to Tell Stories- Level2

"I want to be a leader..a thought leader"- My words

In post Day1037 we talked about Content Awareness as being the first level of telling stories. This level is all about establishing trust(T), being found(BF), and generating greatness(GG). In this post we will move on to level two.

Level two is when a blog creator becomes a **Thought Leader(TL)**.

The first requirement to becoming a Thought Leader is to **Create Trust(CT)**. On level one we established trust and on this level we are creating trust. What is the difference? Either you have trust or you don't? I believe that the difference rests in the time frame. People will give you initially invest in you a small level of trust. If they feel like you deserve it they will increase and the bond will become stronger. I believe that if you have written without abusing this trust for a while, maybe 6 months to a year, you will reach the CT level.

Second requirement of being thought of as a TL is to start to **Meet Demand(MD)**. Your audience will get used to your publishing schedule and pretty soon you will be synchronized. If you publish monthly they will know. If you publish weekly they will tune in weekly. Daily publishing is a challenging but in my opinion it is worth it.

The third requirement for level two is to become an **Efficient Funnel(EF)**. I believe that most people are too busy to dedicate themselves to following anyone. They will sporadically read your work as long as you are able to help they learn something new quickly. They do not want to be sold to and have to read a book every time they show up to your blog. Short and sweet.

With that said, I have started writing slightly longer posts this year. Why? I noticed that the longer ones expressed my ideas better and lead to larger audience. But be careful! Key word here is Efficient.

Unlike level one where you had to move from trust to being found to generating greatness, level two works best as an intersection of these requirements. I will model intersection as ^.

As an equation level two can be modeled as:
$$TL = CT \wedge MD \wedge EF$$

Today's question is:
"Do you want to influence your audience's thoughts?"

Tuesday, December 10, 2013

365QOD- Day1039

How to Tell Stories- Level3

"The ultimate level: Storyteller"- My interpretation of a figure in the book **Epic Content Marketing** by Joe Pulizzi.

Top, third, level in telling stories is to become a **Storyteller(S)**.

First requirement of being classified as Storyteller is to **Create Demand (CD)**. After a while of not abusing the trust that readers have entrusted you with, your audience will grow. But to create demand you have to continue learning and developing in order to share your growth. The demand will not be there if you talk about the same topic every day. If you did that it sounds like preaching instead of sharing something cool with your audience.

As you continue to learn and develop you will start to differentiate yourself. The second requirement of this third level is **Differentiates (D)**. If you sound like someone else then you do not sound like yourself. It is easy to fall in this trap. It is easy and lazy thinking. Read others but think for yourself and provide that difference as the reason for your audience to want to hear your thoughts. Remember that if everyone is thinking the same thoughts then no one is thinking.

Last requirement of the third level is to **Creates Evangelists (CE)**. This is when the audience snowballs your efforts and you experience step change levels in audience numbers. The audience invites others to become members of the audience. You then have Evangelists.

At this level the intersection is so large between these three requirements that it is hard to tell whether you are creating demand, differentiating, or creating evangelists. Or all three at the same time. As an equation, S=function of(CD,D, CE)

As a review, the equations for the three levels are:
$$CD= T + CD + GG$$
$$TL= CT \wedge MD \wedge EF$$
$$S=\text{function of}(CD, D, CE)$$

So where am I? I believe that I am somewhere in the Thought Leader level. But now I realize that I need to improve my differentiation, creating demand, and hopefully convincing evangelists to help me.

Today's question is:
"How good of a storyteller are you?"

Monday, January 13, 2014

365QOD- Day1073

Use of Solitude

"In order to be open to creativity, one must have the capacity for constructive use of solitude. One must overcome the fear of being alone."- Rollo May

I have no fear of being alone. It is not in my nature that I have to have people around me. But I am no hermit. I can be an extrovert or an introvert.

When there is no one around then I become very productive. The idea of constructive solitude is how I recharge. Sitting around on a vacation drains me unless I am doing something creative. The quality of my life is highly dependent on my perceived level of creativity.

I believe that the secret is in having a plan. Usually I know what I need to bring with me to fulfill a specific goal and how long it will take me to do it. If my time is planned then I have less of a temptation to do something wasteful. This is not to say that I do not break my plan but that I work at sticking to it.

Today's question is:

"Do you fear being alone?"

Monday, February 3, 2014

365QOD- Day1093

Twisted

"Unexpected!"- My reaction

Recently I went into Marcus Ashley gallery in Lake Tahoe. I love walking into galleries to see if there are types of works I have never seen before. This gallery did not disappoint. I saw the works of Andrew Gonzalez and Steve Barton.

Andrew's work was ghostly black and white images. They pulled you in because they were unlike anything I have seen before. These were amazing images in black/brown and white.

Steve's work stood out differently. The art was OK by itself. BUT what he did with the art was everything. The canvas was twisted onto a wooden structure. Amazing 3D effect! The images combined with the frame pulled you in.

I would have never created a twisted canvas. Most canvases are flat and the art fools the eye into a 3D look. Steve twisted the given and created a niche. He did not settle for the norm that we all expect.

Today's question is:
"What else is flat that should be twisted?"

Wednesday, February 5, 2014

365QOD- Day1095

Designing an App

"What should I build an app for?"- A good question

According to Gary Vaynerchuk, a social media expert, most people's cell phones contain three types of apps:"

1. Social Networking, which tells you that people are interested in other people
2. Entertainment, including games and music apps, which tells you that people want to escape
3. Utility, including maps, notepads, organizers, and weight loss management systems, which tells you that people value service."

So let us take the three ideas: Social Networking, Entertainment, and Utility and play with them. Suppose we would create an app that combines Social Networking and Entertainment. In other words it could be a game that we learn about other people in a small friends circle by posing a statement that is true about someone in the group that people would figure out who it is.

How about combining Social Networking and Utility? A group weight loss program that allows you to see what everyone is doing would fit that niche.

Suppose we chose Entertainment and Utility. We could have a map of all of the stars in a particular city at one time by using their social presence information. For those who love to track their stars this will allow them to try to meet their stars if they are interested.

The point of this exercise is to show you that one can generate many new ideas by combining features of what people already use. You can see quickly how one can come up with several app ideas that might just take off. The app might be the next Facebook. You don't think so? Who would have thought that 10 years ago Facebook would take off?

Today's question is:

"What app would you design?"

Decision Making

Tuesday, March 5, 2013

365QOD-Day759

"I did it!" - My relief

I went out for a run on January 1, 2013 and felt a pain in my right Achilles tendon. I ran through it and thought that was the end of it.

Well, after coming back home I realized that the pain only temporarily went away. So I decided to give my body a break and take a month off. During this month I will let the body heal itself.

February 1st I tried to run again. My run lasted 1 minute and 30 seconds. I stopped and decided to give myself another month. During this month I started doing yoga and working out on an elliptical machine.

On Sunday March 2nd I went out for a 3 mile run. I ran it and it felt good. My leg muscles were letting me know that I have not pushed them that hard in a while BUT that was a good pain. To tell the truth, I probably ran a little faster than I wanted because on the way back I struck a conversation with another runner. I ran it in 30 minutes.

Today's question is:
"Can you stop hurting yourself in order to let the body heal?"

Sunday, April 7, 2013

365QOD- Day792

"My gut feeling tells me to do X" - often heard expression

Recently I read an article that talked about the difference between analytical and intuitive decision making. One is based on facts and other is based on feelings.

A lot of people make decisions intuitively. They can sense what they believe is the right thing to do and just want to get to the doing stage quickly. The problem with this approach is that often opinions are based on a single past experience.

Other people need a lot of facts and figures. They live to analyze these until they feel 100 percent that they know what the right answer is to the problem. The problem is that you can never get to complete certainty.

In my opinion a blend is the best way to make decisions. It is the 80/20 rule again. I think that once you have 80% knowledge of the facts and figures you have spent enough time analyzing and should stop. Now take a look at the numbers and ask yourself do you feel (20%) that what the numbers are telling you is the right thing to do?

If the answer is yes then pull the trigger and go for it. If you still feel discomfort then search for more data or another approach to solving the problem.

Today's question is:
"Do you know or feel your decisions are correct?"

Thursday, May 30, 2013

365QOD- Day846

"Need at least two valid choices" - my conclusion

I am currently reading a book on decision making by Heath brothers. In the book they mention a study on decision making. The study found that only five percent of the decisions involved three or more choices. The other 95 percent were made up of two types: whether to do something or not (40), two choices (55).

Now it gets interesting. After some time has passed, the decisions got evaluated. Only six percent of the whether to do something or not were correct. 40 percent of the two choice decisions were correct. Overall 46 out of the 95 percent were correct.

In other words, about fifty percent of the decisions were correct. What I learned from that story is that in order to improve we need to have at least two good valid options.

Today's question is:
"Do you have at least two valid options to choose from?"

Friday, May 31, 2013

365QOD- Day847

"Good for what horizon?"- My thought

Often times we just want to make a decision. We just want to get it over. In my opinion this is short term thinking.

There exists a decision making technique called 10/10/10. I believe it was originated by Suzy Welch.

In this technique you consider the effect of the decision
1. 10 minutes from now
2. 10 months from now
3. 10 years from now

Suppose you need to have an uncomfortable conversation with your boss. 10 minutes after the conversation you will still feel uncomfortable but you will be glad that it is over. 10 months from now you will most likely not worry about the effects of that decision. 10 years from now you will most likely not know your boss and could care even less about this decision and conversation. It seems that decision making gets easier when you consider the different timeframes.

Today's question is:
"Do you consider the 10/10/10 effects of your decisions?"

Saturday, June 1, 2013

365QOD- Day848

"Let me tell you a story." - A good beginning

Recently I had a conversation with a friend who worked as a business consultant. Our conversation eventually led to a story of a small company he had worked with through a change and quality improvement efforts.

The company was run by a father who wanted it done his way. The owner had a son who was interested in the effort but his passion was sales. He could sell anything.

The company had some quality issues with which my friend could give them a strategy to solve. It was straight out of a textbook.

However, the effort to change never succeeded. The owner could only see his way as the way to run the company. In other words his approach was purely intellectual. The son was emotional about the sales but not about running the business. There was no clear path on which to place various success milestones along to guide them.

This story confirmed for me the wisdom of the Heath brothers book Switch. In the book the rider (intellectual), the elephant (emotion), and the path (mission) have to align. You must provide incentives on the path that aligns with your thinking and emotions.

My friend tried to connect those pieces for this business. It is my belief that, without knowing the company, ultimately the company will fail. It was not flexible to adapt to new ways.

Today's question is:
" In your change efforts do you align the path, the rider, and the elephant?"

Sunday, June 2, 2013

365QOD- Day849

"My priorities are...."- not so easy to determine

I believe as individuals we often do not know what we want. You would think that priorities would be easy and we can just say them. Unfortunately they are not.

How about in the business world? Should a company know its priorities? The answer is of course. This is often driven from the top executives.

While reading the book on decision making by the Heath brothers I learned of a study conducted by MIT. In the study they asked executives what are their top 5-8 problems. Easy enough.

A week later they came back and asked the executives to review their calendars. Amazingly enough there were no activities on their schedule that connected to the problems they had identified a week before. In other words, we can tell what we should be doing but it does not necessarily mean that we will do it.

Today's question is:
"Does your calendar reflect your priorities?"

Tuesday, June 4, 2013

365QOD- Day851

"The opinion of one is so easy"- Carrie Mathews

I happen to be a leader who is not afraid to be wrong. As a matter of fact I assume that I am wrong until proven right.

Unfortunately, some other "leaders" choose to believe that their input is the only valid input. As a matter of fact, they seek no input.

When leaders do not seek input they do not open themselves up to the wisdom of crowds. Often those top down decisions fail. Failure might not be immediate but it is eminent. As the old saying goes, "Those who do not study history are doomed to repeat it."

A manager who does not get input from his people is simply doomed to repeat the mistakes from the past.

Today's question is:
" How open are you to differing input from others?"

Thursday, June 6, 2013

365QOD- Day853

"Always look for at least one more option "- lesson I learned

I am currently working on a hot project. The operations folks want to buy a replacement in kind for a piece of equipment.

Normally that is pretty easy to do. I challenged my team by asking for an improvement in kind. In other words, what issues can be eliminated by buying a better piece of equipment from the same manufacturer?

I was happy with myself. I changed the whether decision into a better whether decision. However, my balloon was busted by a person when he asked me if the team had considered alternate technology.

Because of the needs of the plant and making the transition quickly, we looked for a replacement from the current equipment manufacturer. But the point is very valid. We should have given ourselves a legitimate second option. We did not. This makes our decision quality poor.

Today's question is:
" How do you force yourself to add a valid second option to your decision?"

Tuesday, July 2, 2013

365QOD- Day879

"Most people only half-heartedly decide they want a lot of things. You have to get really clear on what you really want. The question is how badly do you want it? - Steve Siebold

This quote offers wonderful advice. We tend to want lots of things. But a want is different than need.

I believe the decision has to be full-hearted. With every fiber you must want it. You want it enough to sacrifice something else for it. Then it is a need.

What? If you believe that you can have it all without giving up something, then you are doing things half-hearted. You only have so many minutes in a day to squeeze it all in.

Always figure that one for one you must give up an equal time user to get a new want. Otherwise you are playing mind games with yourself.

Today's question is:
"How do you know that you have made a want truly full hearted?"

Monday, July 8, 2013

365QOD- Day885

"The choices we make, not the chances we take, determine our destiny"-Unknown

While visiting a coworker I noticed a new poster with this caption. I had to write it down before I continued to my meeting.

I believe that the key is the middle portion. To me, it instructs to not take chances but to be strategic with the choices we make. In the end the choices will be our destiny.

However, at times we do not know the right choice and we have to take a chance. This is ok for a few decisions but it cannot be the method by which we select the majority of our decision choices.

Today's question is:
"Do you believe that choices or chances are more important to shaping your destiny?"

Tuesday, July 16, 2013

365QOD- Day892v2

"Fast and roughly right decision-making will replace deliberations that are precise but slow"- Rita Gunther McGrath

I am not a perfectionist. Sometimes I do take the time to make up my mind but that is unusual. I can be swayed by a good argument because I believe that I am wrong until proven otherwise.

From my recent readings on decision making, we should always make sure we have at least two good options to choose from and towards which we are not biased. But once we have those two choices then we need to pull the trigger and make a decision.

The decision that we make will at times need adjusting but we should believe enough in ourselves that we can make those adjustments. The key words in this quote are to aim for a fast decision that is "roughly right" and proceed.

Today's question is:
"How do you make your decisions fast and roughly right?"

Friday, July 19, 2013

365QOD- Day895

"Was a root cause analysis done?"- Bill Brown

The other day I sat in a meeting during which we discussed how our team has been modifying the process of satisfying our customers' requests. The meeting was an eye opener.

During the meeting we discussed how we have transitioned from equipment replacement in kind to improvement in kind. We have been questioning our customers as to what their issues are with their current design. Then our new philosophy evolved into considering alternative solutions.

So we felt pretty good about our evolution. By we also noticed that our costs typically were going up. This is not a bad consequence if our customer's problem is eliminated and the replacement cycle extended.

However, while talking about a specific job Bill asked whether a root cause was identified. We all looked at each other signaling no. In other words, we purchased an expensive piece of equipment that will hopefully resolve the problem but it also might not. Maybe all we did was delay the reappearance of the problem?

Immediately we decided that confirming that the root cause has been identified should be our first step.

Today's question is:
"How do you know that you are solving the right problem?"

Thursday, August 8, 2013

365QOD- Day915

The Road not Traveled

"What if I was wrong?"-a great question

The other day I had a great conversation with a friend about choices. His point of view was that he made a choice in life many years ago and settled. The first thought I had was, "Maybe we should not settle?" Should we?

I believe that settling is very common. For whatever reason we can come up with, at that time, we chose the less difficult road. That road does not lead to a great story.

Unfortunately we only have one life and choosing the safe road mostly makes that one life less memorable. If every day we choose the safe road then we will end up living a life of settlement.

I am reading a book on habits that mentions a story from a book in which the main character uses dice therapy. In this therapy the character chooses what to do amongst several choices by rolling a die. This takes one out of their normal pattern. It definitely would push one to not settle and try different experiences.

In the story it mentions that most of the people around the character had a difficult time adjusting to this change. I believe that such an experience can make us challenge our normal patterns and get out of our box. This will be uncomfortable for us and for those around us. But in the end it might be just what we need.

Today's question is:
"Could you follow dice therapy for a month?"

Friday, August 9, 2013

365QOD- Day916

Stupid Focus

"That is stupid focus" - a management lesson

Recently, I talked about customer service. I also wrote about customer recognition as the next level up.

So what about the opposite side of the customer experience? Recently, I happen to be at an establishment where a manager thought that customer service was customer harassment. It blew my mind.

This manager questioned the validity of the guest's right to be there. When the proof was presented he backed off but then questioned the display of it. On another day instead of remembering the customer he proceeded to question them again.

This is what I call stupid focus. When you do not recognize the customer and create such a stressful experience that the customer chooses not to do business with you. Instead of focusing on making the experience positive his only focus was on rigid rules.

Today's question is:
"How do you prevent stupid focus?"

Wednesday, August 21, 2013

365QOD- Day928

To Lose is to Gain

"One pound per week"- a rule

For three last few weeks I have been trying to lose some weight. This had been very interesting. Difficult might be a better descriptor.

In order to be honest with myself I stated recording everything I eat in an app called MyFitnessPal. I am almost addicted to the app. I enter everything in it religiously. Apparently, I am not the only one.

An article in August 12th issue of UsaToday talks about how apps are beginning to be the popular choice for losing weight. This phenomenon is affecting traditional programs such as weight watchers.
Because of the ease, your friends can join and keep you honest.

One of my coworkers, Carrie, did and she is giving me hell if I slip up or overestimate an exercise. Nothing like an honest critic.

I believe that this is just a part of the quantified self-movement that tries to capture as much information as possible. In the future this might be a bit more automatic through sensors. In the end this app makes it easier for me to track myself.

Today's question is:
"How do you keep yourself on track?"

Sunday, August 25, 2013

365QOD- Day932

Go to School and Then Get a Job.

Q: What is a life changing realization that you wish you'd had sooner?
"The traditional road to education and success is a trap. But it is actually a road. So if you do not take it, you'd better have a damn good alternative routes planned." -unknown

I am way over educated for what I do. But I am educated and can choose to not use most of my education and still get by just fine. So I did choose that road.

What about the roads I did not choose? Ones I did not even entertain. Mainly because I was told when I was young that I well go to college. I had no choice or did I come up with alternatives.

I do believe that the price of education is dropping very quickly. Many graduates are having a hard time finding a job and paying their loans back. The road to success most traveled has a big pot hole. Watch out!

The reality is that kids need to learn how to learn outside of a traditional program and the world would be theirs. If they then choose to go to school they will be better prepared. This was not uncommon in the 50s when many adults who had worked went back to school in the evening. Many older engineers that I worked with had practical experience before filling out their theoretical knowledge when they went back to school. This is what made those old guys great.

Today's question is:
"Do **you always consider alternatives when it comes to life choices or do your go with the obvious choice**?"

Tuesday, October 8, 2013
365QOD- Day976

Scary

"Despite campaigns aimed at educating both clinicians and patients, studies show that hospital staff comply with hand washing periodicals only 50% of the time"-WSJ article

I was reading a Wall Street Journal article about SwipeSense when this statistic caught my attention. Immediately it made me wonder.

Why would people that know that "since 1880s that hand hygiene decreases the risk for infection and transmission from person to person" not follow the requirement? It is a classical gap between knowing and doing.

SwipeSense is providing sensors and gel dispensers designed to analyze and provide an incentive for the staff to follow the protocol. But why is the knowledge not enough.

I believe that in this instance doctors feel that they know more than the rest of us and see themselves as above the rest of us. Even though their oath emphasizes that they do no harm they are doing harm. It is their ego that is driving their decision making.

Today's question is:
"How do you prevent your ego from driving your decisions?"

Thursday, October 24, 2013

365QOD- Day992

Kicking Your Own

"If we were replaced tomorrow, what would our successors do first?"-Andy Grove question to Gordon Moore

Intel was in the memory business. They were the industry leader. But they sensed that the market was changing and that they needed to get out of the memory business. They debated it for a while.

One day while having a conversation Grove and Moore wondered what would their successors do if they were replaced by the board? They both looked at each other and said, "Get out of the memory business. So if they would get out of the memory business, why don't we leave the building, come back in and do the same thing?"

This is an interesting question and deals with how we should all approach our jobs. If we were to be replaced what would be obvious to our successor to change that maybe we should change. Maybe we should change it?

How about on a personal level? The other day I was listening to an old Shark Tank episode in which Mark Cuban said, "I often ask myself, if I wanted to kick my own a$$ what would I do?" I thought that this was a personal version of the other question.

We should always be aware of our weaknesses and how someone could use those against us. Change them, reduce them, and conquer them before they destroy us.

Today's question is:
"How would you kick your own a$$?"

Friday, November 22, 2013

365QOD- Day1021

The Upholder

"Making a habit= Following rules. Some personality types thrive when given rules and some rebel against them. To successfully adapt our habits, we need to be aware of how we deal with rules we impose on ourselves ("inner rules") and rules imposed on us by others ("outer rules")."- Gretchen Rubin Ted speech ideas and author of The Happiness Project and Happier at Home

In next four posts I want to review and discuss what Gretchen defines as four personality types when it comes to habits. In today's post I want to review and discuss the first type: T**he Upholder**.

Ms. Rubin defines **The Upholder** as someone who is great at
1. adhering to inner rules
<u>and</u>
2. adhering to outer rules.

The way I would define this person is someone who has great control of themselves. They are able to self-correct their behavior by setting up inner rules. As an example, it might be a person who chooses to lose weight and they simply decide to not eat dinner. They just stop eating dinner.

But not only are they great at creating their own self rules they follow outer rules equally. In other words, if they are the team leader and their boss tells them to execute X they do not challenge it and simply execute it. This is OK for most unimportant decisions but for critical path changing decisions that is dangerous.

The way I would term the Upholder is someone who is a great follower. Once rules are set up, inner or outer, they just follow.

Today's question is:
"Are you an Upholder?"

Saturday, November 23, 2013

365QOD- Day1022

The Questioner

"And why are we doing this?"- something I often ask

In this second of four posts I want to review and discuss what Gretchen defines as the second of four personality types when it comes to habits. In today's post I want to review and discuss the second type: **The Questioner**.

Ms. Rubin defines **The Questioner** as someone who is great at
1. **adhering to inner rules**
and
2. **questions outer rules.**

The way I would define this person is someone who has great control of themselves. They are able to self-correct their behavior by setting up inner rules. As an example, it might be a person who chooses to take up marathon running. They just start small by running one mile and build up from that point.

They are great at creating and following their own self rules but they question outer rules equally. In other words, if they are the team leader and their boss tells them to execute X they challenge it and will not simply execute it until the reason for the rule is clearly communicated. This often has to be communicated face to face and not through email- an informal form of communication.

The way I would term The Questioner is someone who will make an idea better by questioning its need. Once the reasoning is clear, I believe that the Questioner will follow the outer rule as if they set it up themselves.

Today's question is:
"Are you a Questioner?"

Sunday, November 24, 2013

365QOD- Day1023

The Rebel

"Rebel without a cause."- a movie title

In this third of four posts I want to review and discuss what Gretchen defines as the third of four personality types when it comes to habits. In today's post I want to review and discuss the third type: **The Rebel**.

Ms. Rubin defines **The Rebel** as someone who is horrible at
1. **adhering to inner rules**
<u>and</u>
2. **all outer rules.**

The way I would define this person is someone who has great confidence in themselves. They are out of control when it comes to setting up inner rules. They feel that they need to live in the moment and not create rules of what can and cannot be done. A rebel just does not care if their rules make sense to anyone. Hell, they do not even follow them themselves.

A Rebel cannot follow any outer rules. They tend to believe that they are outside of the hold of any rules set up by someone else. This leads to making many transitions in relationships and jobs. A Rebel is driven by a constant need for a new challenge. In the example I used with the first two types, if they are the team leader and their boss tells them to execute X they ignore it and will simply not execute it.

A rebel has to create their future by working for themselves. They cannot survive in someone else's world.

Today's question is:
"Are you a Rebel?"

Monday, November 25, 2013

365QOD- Day1024

The Obliger

"I feel obligated to..."- a common expression

In this last post on rules I want to review and discuss what Gretchen defines as the last of four personality types when it comes to habits. In today's post I want to review and discuss the forth type: **The Obliger**.

Ms. Rubin defines **The Obliger** as someone who is
1. horrible at adhering to inner rules
but
2. great at following all outer rules.

The way I would define this person is someone who has no confidence in themselves. They never set up rules for themselves. They feel that they are not worthy to create rules. An Obliger cares more about what others want than what they need.

An Obliger follows all outer rules. They tend to believe that rules made by others are better than what they could come up with and they do not challenge any of them. They are the ultimate follower. Unfortunately, many companies love to reward these followers with leadership roles. Why? Because they will not question rules and follow orders. They are the perfect little soldiers. In the example I used with all of the types, if they are the team leader and their boss tells them to execute X they simply do it. Without a moment of doubt that it is the right thing to do.

An Obliger cannot create a future for themselves. They can only survive in someone else's world.

Today's question is:
"Are you an Obliger?"

Friday, January 31, 2014

365QOD- Day1090

Future Perfect People

"When I hire designers, I look for future perfect people. Some people have the potential, but they haven't had the opportunities. Their portfolios are full of mediocre work, but it's not because they're mediocre designers. It's because they've been given mediocre opportunities.

A lot of future perfect people are stuck in current mediocre positions. They just haven't had the chance to do their best work."- Jason Fried, 37Signals

In past posts I argued that the hiring process is faulty. Often as hiring managers we tend to hire copies of ourselves. As I have said it before, that doubles the company's strengths and doubles the company's weaknesses. So I would rather hire individuals that think and do different than me. This gets rid of the echo chamber that a lot of managers enjoy.

So Jason brings up an interesting twist. He bets on the employee being a 'future perfect person.' This is a dangerous bet but if you invest in people I believe he would succeed.

I believe that the key is the investment in making sure they are not stuck in mediocre positions and are nurtured with guidance and training to elevate them to the 'future perfect' level. Most companies fail in either or both of these aspects that lead to success. They have rigid rules for promotions and or no training to help the employee succeed. This is not a symptom at only small companies but also in large global companies. The reason is that it is not a value to a founder/CEO and it never gets engrained in the culture.

Today's question is:

"Are you a future perfect person stuck in a mediocre job?"

Demanding

Wednesday, November 27, 2013

365QOD- Day1026

Nonlinear Life

"Step A then Step B then Step C..."- - the linear plan

As humans we like to plan our lives. We even like to plan the lives of our children. If little Johnny goes to this school, followed by this high school, followed by this college, and then gets a job with a great company he will be set for life. This is an example of linear thinking.

Unfortunately, life is rarely linear. It often forces us to do multiple things at the same time and it feels like our lives are chaotic. This is an example of nonlinear life. In this type of a life, step A does not lead into step B, step B might have to be done in parallel with C, next going for E before backing up to do step D. Most of us fit this type of a life.

So is it wrong to think linearly? Nope. Even in the most chaotic nonlinear life there are linear subsystems. As a matter of fact, while doing my masters level work, I learned that often science tries to treat nonlinear problems by linearizing them. In other words, for a certain range the system is linear. Once that assumption is made and verified then it is easy to use many linear techniques to solve the problem. (The way to visualize this is to think of a curve which on a certain range looks like a line.)

Why is this important? Well, often we feel overwhelmed and in the midst of chaos. Stopping for a moment to ask if some linearity can be found in the chaos might make it more obvious on how to find the right solution. Maybe doing things in parallel, multitasking, seems like a great idea but determining if those two steps could be done sequentially might eliminate the stress while not extending the timeframe by too much.

Today's question is:

"Do you look for opportunities to linearize your nonlinear life?"

Direction

Monday, July 15, 2013

365QOD- Day892

"The greatest thing in the world is not so much where we are, but in what direction we are moving"- Oliver Wendel Homes

In older posts I have referred to the idea of where we are at any moment as our current state. By that I mean the level at which we are along different dimensions such as: physical, mental, emotional, spiritual, financial, interpersonal, focus, discipline, urgency, etc.

The quote above warns that more than the state, which is never ideal, we should focus on the direction we are moving in. For example, if I have not been working out much then my state might be a 3 out of 10. Now I can settle for that level or figure out how to nudge myself to a 4.

The key is to not be content with your current state and to always have a plan on how to move yourself from your current state- current equilibrium. Just by moving a bit you might reach a better equilibrium that is much better than where you are currently.

Today's question is:
"How do you move yourself from your current state?"

Tuesday, July 23, 2013

365QOD- Day899

"I do not have a bucket list but I have a f$ck it list that is a mile long."- Don Amerson

Yesterday I heard another co-worker utter these words and give Don credit. Immediately I formulated a post in my mind.

About a month ago I found an old bucket list from ten years ago. I did nothing with it except sit it on my desk. My idea was to sit down and look at how many of my to do items were done.

Don's wisdom is the reverse side. How many of the bucket list items are on the f$ck it side? In other words not important at all to me as a life goal. Probably there are quite a few.

Maybe scheduling a five year review of the bucket list is a great idea. Five years is a long enough timeframe for me to get some things done and some of the items on the list to need dropping.

Today's question is:
"Which one of your lists is longer?"

Wednesday, August 28, 2013

365QOD- Day935

Apple put the cult in culture

"Before I got to IBM I used to think that culture was important but now I see it is the most critical"-Lou Gersner

Consider these two statements and you should quickly realize that they are describing two different types of culture. One is internal and the other is external.

Gersner must have quickly realized that in order to save IBM from destroying itself he needed to change it from the inside. He could not control what the customer chose to do but he can lead IBM towards a place where the company can thrive. IBM got out of certain businesses that were not successful and focused on its core.

Apple is the other extreme. It built an internal culture on being so hip and cool that the world wanted to join. They were not building computers for the masses but for the cool creative people. If you bought a product you entered into that culture and you became a member of the Apple cult. You drank the cool aid and bought the genius T-shirt.

I believe that Lou only managed to win half the battle. Yes he managed to resurrect a bleeding giant but did not create the cult following. To move to that level you need products that are remarkable. Products worth remarking about.

Today's question is:
"Can you start a cult?"

Sunday, September 22, 2013

365QOD- Day960

Shaping

"One's philosophy is not best described in words; it is best described in the choices one makes. In the long run, we shape our lives and we shape ourselves. The process never ends until we die. And, the choices we make are ultimately our responsibility."-Eleanor Roosevelt

Responsibility is a heavy weird for most of us. We want to take credit for our successes and want to redirect the focus for our failures. It is human nature. If we admit that it was us, then maybe we were not good enough? What a mistake!

As Eleanor points out, it is the choices that are our true philosophy. It is not empty words that we say but do not apply.

So if we want to shape our lives then we have to recognize the results that we do not desire and make better choices in order to get better results. This choosing and making better choices is a never ending process. The process is the basis of my first book, **The Result**.

It is encouraging to know that we do have control and often several choices we can make at any instant. Unfortunately, most often we are not aware of the present enough to consciously choose. So the key, in my opinion, is to become more consciously aware at each moment in order to choose the best option that will lead us towards our ultimate self.

Today's question is:
"Do you actively shape your life through your choices?"

Friday, January 24, 2014

365QOD-Day1084

Dream Job vs. Current Job

"Would you apply to your current job today? If you answered 'no,' then you're among the 50% of executives today who feel disengaged, unchallenged and stuck in the wrong job.* As the New Year begins, now is the best time to stop wasting time in the wrong position — and take action."- ExecuNet email content

In my opinion, for most people, this question is very dependent on the state of the economy. During down times people would just keep their heads down and just work. This is when employers have an advantage.

But when times get better and opportunity starts to return then the desire for a change and to do better starts rising to the top. As the quote points out, they "feel disengaged, unchallenged, and stuck in the wrong job" so changing to a better job becomes a must.

The reason I titled this post dream job vs. current job is to point out that often the jump is not to a dream job but to a 'better' job. It might be the better pay. It might be the less hectic hours. It might be the new co-workers, etc. Whatever it is the change might not be to our ideal job. It just might be a slight improvement over our current one.

Remember that we often make decisions for two reasons: to avoid pain or to get more pleasure. So when evaluating anything new, ask yourself if you are trying to avoid pain or trying to get more pleasure? This first decision lets you know if you have the right reason for wanting to make a change.

Today's question is:

"Would you apply to your current job today?"

Saturday, January 25, 2014

365QOD-Day1085

Measuring the Right Things

"Are you measuring the right thing?"- Steven J. Thompson

Our worlds are full of data. It is only going to get worse. With smaller and smaller sensors and cheaper and cheaper storage, we will have more and more access to all kinds of data. The conversion from data to information is the next level. Even though this conversion is critical to improving, it is often not done or done effectively. So we just collect data and do nothing with it.

So if we are collecting data and not obtaining useful information from it, then why bother collecting it in the first place. Steven also teaches us that, **"In almost any data-gathering situation, there are far more types of information that could be gathered than you can possibly tackle. Compare the contradictory claims that U.S. wireless phone providers make for their network coverage. No one's lying--they're all just picking different aspects of coverage to measure."**

In other words we might diligently collect the wrong data. As the example illustrates, even if we did obtain information from it, the information would lead us to the wrong conclusion. This is worthless!

We would be better off if we make sure we are measuring the right thing and then forcing ourselves to extract information. This would minimize the effort and storage, and maximize the understanding of the results.

Today's question is"

"How do you know you are measuring the right thing?"

Doing

Wednesday, February 13, 2013

365QOD- Day739

"Only 5 percent of entrepreneurship is the big idea, the business model, the whiteboard strategizing, and the splitting up of the spoils. The other 95% is
the gritty work that is measured by innovation accounting: product priorit ization decisions, deciding which customer to target or listen to,
and having the courage to subject a grand vision to constant testing and feedback."- Lean Startup book

Man if I can only come up with a billion dollar idea! Does this sound like you?

Most people believe if they can only get one idea their lives would be set. This lack of an idea is followed by realization that one is lacking, time, money, etc. to execute the idea properly.

But as the quote states the idea is only 5% of the battle. Unfortunately we stop at the 5% and never proceed to action and innovation.

The sad part is that ideas are cheap and easy to get. It is not the idea that counts but the execution of that idea. There are many 'poor' smart people with ideas but they never execute any of them.

Today's question is:
"Can you execute the other gritty 95%?"

Saturday, March 16, 2013
365QOD- Day770

"You Only Got Video Game"- t-shirt slogan

I am a believer in not claiming expertise in anything unless you have truly done it. I am surrounded by people who think otherwise.

I have had people claim that they are something that they have never directly done. They might have been around people who were the doers and they simply observed.

The t-shirt slogan above brings forth a new version. Is simulation the same as actually doing it? Some might claim that it is as good. I disagree. Simulation is good training but it can never replace the real thing.

Don't believe me? Imagine getting on a plane and when everyone is seated the captain comes on and says, "Welcome everybody. I am your captain. I have 10000 hours of simulation behind me and this is my first flight" How comfortable do you feel as you buckle up?

Today's question is:
"What kind of game do you have?"

Friday, April 12, 2013

365QOD - Day797

"Big ideas are just that- ideas- until you execute"- Kristina "Z" Holly

It is amazing how many ideas I can get by just reading a magazine. Let just say I can get 2-3 ideas from each magazine I read. If I want more ideas then I simply just need to read more magazines or books.

The ideas that I get are how to apply an existing idea to another field, modification of an existing idea, or something new that was inspired from the story. In the end the idea is like a dot on a paper. If it is not connected to anything else, it loses any meaning and with time it fades.

It all boils down to the execution of a subset of meaningful ideas to the best of your abilities. Some are quick hits and others take a long time to nurture. Until they bear fruit they are just ideas.

Today's question is:
"What subset of ideas are you going to execute?"

Saturday, July 6, 2013

365QOD- Day883

"Now tear my idea and design apart"- My words of encouragement

The other day I sat in a park with a few friends. One of my friends is a design expert.

A couple of years ago I shared a design idea with him for a product. He told me why the idea did not make sense. Immediately I could tell that what he was telling me would not work in the marketplace.

So for the last two years I have been working on the concept from different angles. I now believe that I am close to the final version of the concept before I manufacture it. With this in mind, I asked Nikolai for his opinion by asking him to be brutal.

He questioned me as to why I believed in the idea. We brainstormed some names for the product. But never did he express his disapproval or doubt of success. Even after he left the group he sent me a text encouraging me to pursue it.

I now believe my idea is ready for the market. It took two years of simmering for it to cook properly.

Today's question is:
"How do you know when your idea has reached the perfect time for execution?"

Entrepreneur

Friday, March 8, 2013

365QOD-Day762

"A One-Acre Farm in a 320 Square Foot Box"- title of an article

I recently read two articles about how companies have figured out how to use a 320 square foot shipping container with LEDs, climate controls, and hydroponics in order to be able to produce 900 heads of leafy greens per container each week. The cost of the one company's containers are $60,000.

Wow!

I am not impressed with the price but the idea of re-using the containers. The cost of old used containers cannot be much. Let's go with $1000. To outfit it with the electronics and necessary tools to make it functional, probably another 9k. All together maybe $10,000 would do the trick.

So if you can create a way for someone to buy up a bunch of containers, update them and place them in inner cities on old lots that have a power and water connection, you could turn a profit pretty quickly.

Today's question is:
"What other uses besides gardening could old containers be put to use?"

Wednesday, March 20, 2013

365QOD- Day774

"You wrote an app?" - An innocent inquiry

I recently published my first app. So what?

Marketing it is everything. I recently read these four questions that an app developer needs to answer:
1. Who are your competitors?
Looking through the academy app section I did not see anything close to it.

2. What are the key features of your app?
In one app it teaches theory, provides complete examples, and a tool for further learning.

3. What are the benefits of your app?
User can learn the theory, application, and experiment with a topic by playing with the app.

4. What is unique about your app?

The unique mix of theory, application, and tool to learn a subject.

Today's question is:
"How would you answer these questions for your product or service?"

Thursday, March 21, 2013

365QOD- Day775

"What are the differences?" - An obvious question

Recently I looked through a book called the ***Top 10 Distinctions Between Entrepreneur and Employees.*** The title made me pose the question. I am going to start a new label: entrepreneur for the blog. Why start a label? Under business I will focus more on business actions and in this new label I will focus on applying new business thinking. Let us discuss each of the ten distinctions.

Distinction#1: Entrepreneurs educate themselves more than they entertain themselves. Employees entertain themselves more than they educate themselves.

I believe that this distinction is right on the money. In my opinion we always have to be aware of our gaps. If something is important to your success then determine the gap between where you are and where you want to be when you become successful. Now that you have identified the gap then determine what education will fill that gap. It could be a course, it could be a book, and it could be anything that helps reduce the gap.

The second portion in the distinction is that employees entertain themselves. If you spend your time at work and at home watching TV or just surfing the web then you are not educating yourself. It is a choice.

Today's question is:
"What are you educating yourself to do?"

Friday, March 22, 2013

365QOD- Day776

"Knowing the difference is half the battle"- Anonymous

Continuing with our distinctions series:

**Distinction#2: Entrepreneurs have an empowering perspective of failure.
          Employees see failure as bad.**

This distinction fits well with my beliefs. My first book, **The Result**, defines that there is no such thing as failure but a result that we need to nudge towards our definition of success. By believing this, one allows oneself to be empowered instead of being focused on failure. This results in continuous improvement and increase in confidence.

The second portion of this quote is the belief that many people and employees have is that failure is bad. By placing it in a good vs. bad frame of mind the idea of improving the result is non-existent.

Today's question is:
"Are you empowered by failure?"

Saturday, March 23, 2013

365QOD- Day777

"777 is a lucky number!" - A common belief

Distinction#3: Entrepreneurs are solution finders.
       Employees are problem solvers.

I watched a series a while back about a few men that changed America. This series took a look at some of the giants titans at the end of last century. Titans such as: Vanderbilt, Rockerfellow, Ford, JP Morgan, and Carnegie.

The series educated me that often these guys were not looking to solve a small problem BUT looking to create industries. It was not by luck that they created these industries.

Maybe I am wrong about that? Maybe they started by trying to solve a single problem and then generalized it to create an industry. They were looking for a solution to a need that society had.

Vanderbilt was looking for a way to cheaply transfer goods across the nation so he started the railroad industry. Rockefeller started oil and gas. Carnegie created the steel industry. Morgan the finance industry.

Today's question is:
"Are you focused on the solution or the problem?"

Sunday, March 24, 2013

365QOD- Day778

"I am a generalist. If I need a specialist I hire one" - paraphrase of Henry Ford's words during a trial

Distinction#4 Entrepreneurs know a little about a lot.
         Employees know a lot about a little.

I remember reading a version of the above quote many years ago. It made me realize that if I wanted to be someone who runs companies to be more of generalist than a specialist. To me understanding the big picture while being able to execute it is deep enough. If I am completely focused on the execution then I am becoming a specialist.

Over the years I have stayed away from corporate ladder climbing. I want to get paid what I believe is in line with the specialist position I hold but be given the time outside of work to pursue creating my own ladder.

I believe that I know a lot. Sometimes I feel like I will never know enough. Would I claim mastery of many work processes? Absolutely not! I know enough about a lot.

Today's question is:
"Do you know a little about a lot OR a lot about a little?"

Monday, March 25, 2013

365QOD- Day779

"The sandwich method" - technique for offering a correction

**Distinction#5 Entrepreneurs give and receives praise and correction.
Employees don't praise and try to avoid correction.**

I enjoy praising my co-workers. If praised, I try to re-direct the praise towards my team. If need be, I often use the sandwich method to offer correction.

The sandwich method consists of giving praise, followed by the correction, and lastly ending it with praise. This takes away the defensiveness and allows the person to hear the correction without being defensive.

I find that most employees are insecure and seldom give praise as if praising takes away from them. And God knows they hate any corrections. Correction for me is simply feedback on what I need to improve on. It is information that I can use to get better. I do not take it personal unless it is offered by someone I do not trust.

Today's question is:
"Do you avoid correction?"

Tuesday, March 26, 2013

365QOD- Day780

"I am responsible"- My admission

Distinction#6: Entrepreneurs say, "The buck stops here."
Employee says, "It is not my fault."

I allow the construction supervisors that work for me a lot of freedom. They are allowed to make decisions as if I made them. The main reason I allows this is that a good decision right now is better than a perfect decision much later.

I delegate BUT I also accept the fault when the decision turns out to be a poor one. I have to in order to retain the trust and not to introduce doubt in their decision making.

It is hard to admit fault when someone else makes the decision BUT I believe that as the boss you have to accept the blame if you are to share the successes.

Today's question is:
"Can you take the fall for someone else's decision?"

Wednesday, March 27, 2013

365QOD- Day781

Distinction #7 Entrepreneurs build wealth.
          Employees get paid.

One of the secrets to building a nest egg is getting rid of your debt. Most debt pulls you down into a cycle of working for someone else forever. Good debt is an investment into your future.

An example of good debt could be the decision to get a college degree. If you choose a good major then you are rewarded with a future in which you can repay your loans quickly and start to grow your nest egg.

Another example of good debt would be purchasing a tool. The tool is then used to increase your earning potential.

Example of bad debt is buying a fancy car to impress others. So instead of buying a reasonably priced vehicle which can be paid off immediately, you choose a vehicle that you pay on for years. You are car rich and life poor. You have a car but no money to do anything else.

Today's question is:
"Are you building wealth or earning a paycheck?"

Thursday, March 28, 2013

365QOD- Day782

Distinction#8: Entrepreneurs fly with eagles
	Employees peck around with chickens.

Not the prettiest of distinctions but it will do. The idea here is that when trouble hits you do you rise above it or do you wallow in it.

An eagle rises above the trouble. If there is a gust of wind the eagle uses to rise above it. In other words adversity is converted into an advantage.

An employee sees trouble and wallows in it. It could last a day, week, months, and sometimes the rest of their career. They cannot let go of problems and move on.

Today's question is:
"Do you know how to rise above it?"

Friday, March 29, 2013

365QOD- Day783

"Have you ever driven a car while only looking at the rear view mirror?" - A silly question

**Distinction#9 Entrepreneurs look into the future.
Employees look into the past.**

Your past decisions and experiences have made you in the person who you are today. Stop and spend time understanding your current state. The pause is important.

BUT after you understand what got you to here then focus on the present and future only. Work on your business in the now and once in a while look up to see where you are heading.

The 80/20 rule comes in handy. Spend 20% understanding the past and the other 80%- 60% in doing the present, and 20% looking forward to the future.

Today's question is:
"What percent of your thinking time do you spend in the past, present, and future?"

Saturday, March 30, 2013

365QOD- Day784

The last distinction is:

Distinction#10 Entrepreneurs take risks because of faith.
         Employees play it safe because of fear.

If you do not believe in yourself then it will be difficult to get anyone else to believe in you. Why would they?

Other people will like you and love you, BUT your lack of faith in yourself will not inspire them to have faith when you do not have it.

I always visualize a circle with a line splitting it in half vertically. On the left side is fear. On the right there is faith. We have to nudge ourselves to be on the right side. Start with small decisions and ideas and get some success behind you then your faith will grow.

Today's question is:
"How do you stay in the rights side of the circle?"

Thursday, April 11, 2013

365QOD - Day796

"When life gives you lemons, make lemonade"- an old saying

In March 2013 issue of Entrepreneur I read the story **Shine on** about Josh Opperman. In the story Josh had given a $10,000 ring to his fiancée. One day when he returned home he found out that she had left him and left the ring behind.

I am sure this was a hard experience to go through but Josh did something unusual about it. He took the ring and tried to get his money back. He was offered 35% of its true value. This was not acceptable to Josh so he started a business online to re-sell engagement rings.

Why did I think this was interesting? Well, it made me wonder, "How many businesses can be created off the idea of re-selling something of value for which the original seller will not offer close to true value for?" I always thought that driving a car off the lot and it being worth $2000 less is pretty sick.

A business could be very successful if they would just split the difference with the seller. If an item is bought for 10000 and they can only get 4000 for it then if you split the difference (10000-4000=6000 then 6000/2=3000) and can offer that person 7000 they would purchase from you. Even if you offered them 6000 and you pocketed the 1000 they would sell to you instead of the original seller. You can then re-sell it for 7000.

I think the idea is powerful. Now the trick is to figure out a business in which to use it.

Today's question is:
"What can you re-sell for others?"

Monday, May 6, 2013

365QOD- Day822

"Who are the people shaking up their field most dramatically? To answer that question, we sifted through hundredths of names in scores of categories to come up with a dozen disrupted less content to improve the status quo than to blew it up." Forbes April 15 issue

Usually a hook like this over promises but falls to deliver. But this story did not.

The first disruptor was a company Snapchat which has managed to do something pretty unique. They realized that when we send photos it might be desirable if the photo has an expiration date- "self-destruct ".

It made me wonder if other things should have a self-destruct ability. First thought that came to my mind was email.

What would happen to email traffic if people knew that after 24 hours the email would destroy itself? Maybe people would follow up with a conversation?

Today's question is:
" What else should self-destruct?"

Sunday, May 12, 2013

365QOD- Day828

"Check this out...." - an urging

Recently I started reading an eBook called **Laptop Millionaire**. I started reading the book but quickly realized I needed to stop and create a product. I also ordered the book on order to be able to work with it a little easier than an eBook.

So when I got it in my hand I thought ok now nothing will stop me from reading and working with it. Well, I got a call from my favorite library in town that a new book came in for me.
The book *Contagious by Jonah Berger* has been in front of me the last week. Its focus is on determining what makes ideas go viral. In order took make the ideas memorable it uses the acronym STEPPS.

First idea from the book is that what makes ideas **Spreadable** is that the person who spreads the idea wants to increase their Social Currency. In other words, by spreading the idea the person's image gets a boost.

In a sense the purpose of this blog is to increase my Social Currency. By posting content that folks want to read I am hoping to be recognized as a creative thought leader who can absorb a lot of ideas and make them approachable. In other words, we share things that make us look good in the minds of others.

Today's question is:
" **How do you increase your Social Currency?**"

Monday, May 13, 2013

365QOD- Day829

"Top of mind, tip of tongue"- Contagious book

Second thing to keep in mind when trying to make an idea viral is to consider **Triggers.**

Think of a trigger as a memory device. If a cue is presented, would it trigger a memory or a response?

Consider if someone says peanut butter. What is the first thing that comes to mind? For most of us it would be jelly.

What about if you need to blow your noise? What would you ask for? Most likely, you would ask for a Kleenex.

Today's question is:
" What triggers in your customers mind when you or your product/service are mentioned?"

Tuesday, May 14, 2013

365QOD- Day830

"To keep a fire going, put some kindle in it." - Old advice from my grandmother

In my opinion the most important thing to align in order to make sure something gets done is emotions. The how is easy but the why is hard.

In order for the why to be bigger than the how, you need to do something to get your emotions moving you in the right direction. You would do the same to get an idea to become viral.

According to Contagious book **Emotions** are necessary in order to make an idea viral. What will inspire people to talk about it? What will kindle the emotions? What emotion will move people to act?

Today's question is:
" **What will ignite feelings towards you or your product?**"

Wednesday, May 15, 2013

365QOD- Day831

"Build to show, built to grow"- from the book Contagious

The fourth important feature for an idea or product to become viral is for it to **make it obvious to the Public**.

In the book the example of Apple cover logo being upside down vs. right side up is highlighted. Apple logo is upside down to the user but when the cover is open the logo shows up properly to the public around the user. This is pretty strategic. If it was the other way around then the user is happy for a minute but the public wonders why the logo is upside down.

By placing the logo that way the user's computer provides free advertising to the nearby users that the user prefers the apple brand.

Today's question is:
" Do you built to show?"

Thursday, May 16, 2013

365QOD- Day832

"Now that is useful to know"- something I always say

According to the **Contagious** book, the fifth component of making an idea viral is for it to have **Practical Value**.

I used to be an academic. But I never published papers. I have been credited as author on a few papers but not as a sole author. Publishing academic papers was never of interest to me.

I love writing books and my blog. I believe that these contribute practical ideas to the world. Writing a paper that stretches some theory a little bit is cool but of limited practical value.

So if your idea is of practical value then it has a chance. People have to judge it as something of value that can be applied immediately.

Today's question is:
" How practical is your idea?"

Friday, May 17, 2013

365QOD- Day833

"Let me tell you a story..."-typical beginning

Can you retell the story of the Trojan horse? Most of us had heard it in school somewhere along the way and can probably retell it just as well many years later.

The last idea from the book Contagious is to tell a **Story**.

I'm a believer that a great story can move people to action. But as many greatly entertaining ads illustrate often they do not tie back to the product. The story must connect back to you. The Trojan story links back to the Greeks who built it. The story has a purpose and in the end it links back.

Today's question is:
" **What in the story you tell links back to you?**"

Monday, June 3, 2013

365QOD- Day850

"There are still many opportunities."- My conclusion

Recently I read about a company that found an innovative way to do email on mobile devices. They replaced many of the email functions with Swypes.

They were recently bought for 110 millions. Wow!

What this story teaches me is that there are some new opportunities that have been created by people using smart phones. We just have to keep our eyes open to how people work and how to make it easier for them.

Today's question is:
"How have things changed on smart phones for you and how can you turn that into an opportunity?"

Wednesday, June 5, 2013

365QOD - Day852

"Great entrepreneurship is in the execution. Rare does the initial idea dictate the outcome- perhaps never. Success is about the thousands of ideas and decisions that are made along the way and the speed at which those insights are implemented according to customer needs and feedback." - Eric Paley

While reading an Inc. article by Eric I immediately saw the wisdom being offered. It is about executing and getting feedback from your customers.

Unfortunately, we trend to generate solutions for needs that are at best wants or nonexistent. Eric urges entrepreneurs to:
"**Focus more on falling in love with the problems they want to solve rather than their initial ideas.**

As founders dig deeply into that original hypothesis, they well learn, adapt, hit walls, adapt again, and build critical expertise that they never considered when starting out."

This is the main idea of my first book, **The Result**. It is not about the single idea. It is not about the single moment that you generated it. The process is very iterative and adaptive. Eric advises to see the process as:"
Great entrepreneurs build their success over time, not in a single moment. Ideas are static. Entrepreneurship is dynamic."

Today's question is:
" Can you dynamically iterate and adapt your idea?"

Sunday, June 9, 2013
365QOD- Day856

"pearls.com" - cool site name

While looking through a magazine I red a story about pearls.com. It is a site that provides access to experts to answer your question.

The suite does a review of the person's qualifications so that the answer is valid. It provides that access for a fee.

Many years ago I was teaching a business class on ebusiness. During the class I offered an idea that people and businesses would be willing to pay to get an answer to a difficult problem.

Sometimes businesses do not know how to solve a problem. If a site could assure quality, like pearls.com, then people can bid on solving the problem. This would open it up worldwide, reduce the cost, and increase the quality.

I still think that there is validity to making the process open to bids from several people.

Today's question is:
" **Would you pay someone to solve a business problem you are struggling with?**"

Thursday, June 13, 2013

365QOD- Day860

"I am leaving."- Greg

Today I had a meeting with Greg. He is a young chemical engineer that works in our chemical plant.

Before the meeting he told me that he is leaving. The energy market is very hot so I would not be surprised if he left for a better deal. So I asked him where is he going. His response was surprising, "California, to join a startup".

Those words would imply he had landed a job but not in Greg's world. He wants to go out to California and look around for a startup to join. He figures he can always go back to a chemical plant.

Being a young and single gives Greg the flexibility to be aggressive about his future. It is wise that he wants to see what else the world has to offer. If he would have stayed he would have become a better process engineer but by leaving he will learn how to be an entrepreneur.

I wish his future to be brighter than he believes it will be.

Today's question is:
" **How far on a limb could you go out on?**"

Wednesday, July 24, 2013

365QOD- Day900

"For God's sake, make a decision"-a frustrated urging

I recently read an article by Andrea Huspeni in which she talks about EDP (entrepreneurship dimension profile). This is a 72 question survey that evaluates a person along 14 variables to establish the person's level of entrepreneurship.

The first of the fourteen entrepreneurship variables is: **Independent**.

Being independent means that a person likes to have control of their time, priorities, work, direction, etc. The definition of independence is pretty personal.

So how does one become more independent? Start by making small decisions in an area of importance without anyone's input. Then increase the importance of the decisions. Over time your independence and decision making should improve.

Today's question is:
"Are you independent?"

Thursday, July 25, 2013

365QOD- Day901

"Float like a butterfly, sting like a bee." - Mohammed Ali

Second out of fourteen EDP entrepreneurship dimensions is: **Preference for little structure**

Last night I got a call from a friend. He was asked to teach a course completely outside of his specialty. My friend was not sure whether to teach it or not.

In my career I have instructed many courses including the course he was asked to teach. And guess what, it was also outside of my area of specialty. But my reaction was very different.

I always figured that not knowing the subject provided a great opportunity to stretch myself. I would guess that majority of the courses I have instructed in my career I never took while in school.

This lack of background, and structure on which to build on, caused me to focus and work harder to figure out how to best teach and apply the material. I always believed in myself that I would figure it out. All I needed was a little head start ahead of the students.

Today's question is:
"Do you seek out situations where you know very little or the structure is not well defined?

Friday, July 26, 2013

365QOD- Day902

"I break the mold."- My words

I have never filled the yes man position too well. Why? I like to think for myself.

Third out of fourteen entrepreneurship dimensions is being a **Nonconformist**.

It is amazing to me how corporate cultures tend to breed conformity. Most bosses usually want their employees to not talk back and just follow orders just like the military.

Over time the people that get promoted are people that think alike. One day the CEO realizes that the company is trouble. When the CEO asks for new ideas all that CEO hears is an echo of his thoughts.

Today's question is:
"Are you a nonconformist?"

Saturday, July 27, 2013

365QOD- Day903

"No risk, no gain."- My version

Fourth dimension of EDP is being a **Risk Taker**.

I love my version of no pain, no gain. Risk is often associated with pain. Because the result is not predictable we often choose the darkest ending.

But often we are wrong. The dark ending never comes. Some unpredictable result occurs that we could never imagine even we spent a long time guessing.

So why is being a risk taker important? It moves us away from an equilibrium which is our current state of comfort. That movement has to be big *enough to get momentum to get to a better place. But the risk has to be small enough that it nudges you forward and* with it gives you confidence.

If the leap is too big it could lead to a failure. So make a leap step, control the result, learn from it, and then repeat.

An example of a failure to follow this procedure is when someone first learns to trade stocks. The usually experience success- a beginners luck. What happens next is very interesting. They start taking huge risks that they cannot afford. These unreasonable leaps lead to failure.

Today's question is:
"Do you take small controllable risks?"

Sunday, July 28, 2013

365QOD- Day904

"Action!"- A director's call

Fifth dimension of entrepreneurship according to EDP is being **Action Oriented**.

Many posts ago I write several posts about the GOSPAL goal planning technique. It stands for:
Goal
Objectives
Strategies
Planning
Action
Learning

Notice that everything above action is inside the mind. The action is of special type. It is of the daily action type. Every day you must take an action towards your ultimate goal. Every day!

The everyday actions have to be small enough that they can be accomplished within one day without overwhelming us. While we get these small things accomplished we must be aware enough to learn from these small experiences. This is the L in GOSPAL.

Today's question is:
"Are you action oriented?"

Monday, July 29, 2013

365QOD- Day905

"I lost total track of time."- My words

The sixth dimension of being an entrepreneur according to ETD is **Passion**.

Recently I read an article about how we need to block out our work times in 90 minute blocks. After we get our mental work done, we need to recharge by doing something physical and snacking on something healthy.

I am beginning to believe that there is magic in these ninety minute blocks. Maybe one of these blocks could be used to pause and figure out what makes you tick. What interests you? What bothers you? What problem in front of you needs a solution?

Most of us can probably not spend ninety minutes in a pause state. It is easy to say but difficult to do. Maybe start with five minutes and build up from there. But you do have to start in order to build your passion muscle.

Today's question is:
"What are you working on that makes you lose track of time?"

Tuesday, July 30, 2013

365QOD- Day906

"Do it backwards."-a puzzle solving technique

EDP's seventh entrepreneur dimension is being a **High-Achiever**.

Dick Fosbury is the inventor of the modern high jump. Before him all participants choose to do high jumps by trying to go head first facing the bar. Since him no one jumps facing the bar.

Dick realized a simple fact. The height that he could achieve by turning at the last moment and pushing off was greater than the height that could be achieved when facing the bar and pushing off the toes.

I am sure that the first time he did this technique in competition people scratched their heads in disbelief. But interestingly by doing it backwards he was able to do better than it had ever been done before.

Long time ago I got addicted to solving metal puzzles. I noticed that when I used to solve these puzzles in order to master the puzzle I had to learn how to put the puzzle back into original state. By going backwards I forced myself to slow down and I could solve the puzzle faster in forward direction. I often gave this advice to new puzzle solvers trying to solve the puzzle.

Today's question is:
"Can you do your most important task backwards?"

Wednesday, July 31, 2013

365QOD- Day907

"You cannot drive forwards by looking in a rear vie mirror."- Wise advice

Eight entrepreneurship dimension according to EDP is being **Focused on the Future**.

While driving it is natural to look back once in a while. These times are usually during transitions from one lane to another or to verify that no policeman is following behind us.

Looking back is necessary but it takes away out focus from the direction we are moving on. Often times looking back is done to review past errors and to make sure we do not repeat the mistake.

I believe that a better strategy is to create smaller steps and milestone targets towards our goal. Once in a while look back and establish where we had gone without conflict. But keep moving forward at least 80 percent of the time.

Today's question is:
"How do you stay future focused and minimize the review of past errors?"

Thursday, August 1, 2013

365QOD- Day908

"Eureka!" -words of excitement

The ninth dimension that EDP entrepreneurship test measures is: **Idea Generator**.

I get ideas all of the time. When I am aware I capture those in a word document in order to remember the idea. This way I can pick up the idea and add to it.

So what? Well just because I generate an idea it does not mean that I will execute it. If I had executed every idea I got then I would have been a multi-millionaire by now.

Good ideas are very cheap and easy to come up with. Having great ideas is better. If you're lacking an idea then simply read some magazines in the field of interest and you will find a lot of great new ideas or generate modifications to these great ideas.

However, I do not believe that idea generation is a problem for most people. I believe that idea execution is the problem. Once you have an idea or you borrowed an idea for creating, you must set a time frame when you will get that idea executed.

I love working in three month increments. At this rate I can execute four ideas per year. This may not seem like a lot but I believe it would be a challenge for most people to do better.

Today's question is:
"Which four ideas will you execute this year?"

Friday, August 2, 2013

365QOD- Day909

"Think, execute, execute, execute, and execute" -a great ratio

The tenth EDP dimension is: **Ability to Execute**.

In last post I talked about how important it is to generate ideas and execute those ideas. In this post I want to focus more on the ability to execute.

Just because you can't do something now does not mean that you cannot obtain the skills necessary to be able to do it soon. I believe that this is a critical realization. There will always be a gap between what you can do what you want to do, how you fill the gap is the magic.

We happen to live in a time when information is abundant. Take advantage of the resources that are available online and you can learn anything. You just have to be willing and open to learn.

I believe that the ability to learn and ability to execute are very related. You must force yourself to create a time frame within which you will learn and execute the idea. You have to be gentle with yourself as you might not make all your time frames. As long as you come close within the time frame in the long run it won't make a difference if you execute in three months or three and a half months.

Today's question is
"How good is your ability to execute the new idea?"

Saturday, August 3, 2013

365QOD- Day910

"That is the opposite of what I believe."-my words

The eleventh EDP dimension is: **Self Confident**.

This morning I had a conversation with one of my friends. It was an eye opener.

He spent considerable time talking about the choices he made throughout his career. Most of the stories revolved around the idea of working hard for a boss who eventually gets promoted. The boss then quickly forgets what you did to help them get there.

The thread was that he looked to his bosses as being more of leaders than he believed he was. He would constantly step in and rescue the boss but never achieved the leader post. My friend is a great leader who excels in being a great follower.

I am the opposite. There had never been any doubt in my mind that I can be a great follower if I had a great leader to follow. But unfortunately most of my bosses had a leadership level below me. It is pretty difficult to follow a lesser leader. If you are an average leader, 7 out of 10, you will not follow someone who is a 6 on a leadership scale willingly.

Today's question is:
"**How self-confident are you?**"

Sunday, August 4, 2013

365QOD- Day911

"While you were arguing if the glass is half full (Optimist) or half empty (Pessimist), I drank it"- the Opportunist

The twelfth entrepreneur dimension according to EDP is being an **Optimist**.

I believe that we have to be aware of the negative thoughts and ideas that enter our minds. We have to be the guardians of our mind fortress. Always looking for bad intruders while being slightly paranoid.

Being an Optimist is important. It helps to motivate us to push forward and to believe that tomorrow will be better than today. We have to deal with what is in front of us but not allow it to drag us down by making false generalizations. These generalizations tend to last forever. We need am expiration date for our beliefs.

I believe that the Optimist and Opportunist combination is the best way to attack the future. Be positive but push yourself to take advantage of what is in front of us.

Today's question is:
"Are you an optimistic opportunist?"

Monday, August 5, 2013

365QOD- Day912

"I am persistent." -One of my power slogans I repeat during my runs

EDP's thirteenth dimension is being **Persistent.**

I am trying to lose some weight. I let myself go and got up to 229.6 pounds. Crazy!

So starting with July 16th I woke up and started paying attention to my weight. The first week I added yoga in the morning and evening. In the same time I started eating better and recording all the food I eat and exercises using the Myfitness app. The result was 223 pounds by July 22.

Not happy with this level I then added running up and down a hill for 36 minutes and eventually got up to 72 minutes. How? By repeating my power slogan sentences like the one above.

July 29 I morning weighted myself at 215. Impressive! But I am not done. This week has been a week of plateau. I have jumped up to 218 and down to 216. Losing weight is not linear. The body does not always respond immediately.

So what is my goal? 200 by end of August. Crazy? Yes! But with persistence I will accomplish it.

Today's question is:
"How persistent can you be?"

P.S. I did not achieve my goal.

Tuesday, August 6, 2013

365QOD- Day913

"You are so sensitive."- Supposedly a bad characteristic

According to EDP the fourteenth entrepreneur dimension is **Low Interpersonal Sensitivity**. This one threw me for a loop. Why low? Shouldn't an entrepreneur be sensitive to the people around them? Well it seems the opposite is true for most.

Most likely cause for this insensitivity is their drive towards results. They are focused on results and not people unless those people help them get closer to their goal. Entrepreneurs are results driven.

Is this a bad thing? In my mind you can always be nice to everyone. You do not have to destroy people on your way to the top. Maybe I am wrong and would score low on this dimension. Maybe this is limiting me? It not something that I will change.

Today's question is:
"How insensitive are you to what others say and ask?"

Wednesday, August 7, 2013

365QOD- Day914

"14 posts....that is a long series"-my thought

The last couple of weeks we focused on Andrea Huspeni's article on EDP's dimensions of successful entrepreneurs:
1 independent
2 preference for little structure
3 nonconformist
4 risk taker
5 action oriented
6 passionate
7 high achiever
8 focused on the future
9 idea generator
10 ability to execute
11 self-confident
12 optimistic
13 persistent
14 low interpersonal sensitivity

At this point I believe that the best thing we can do is to be brutally honest and self-assign a score from 1(low level)to 10(high level). The maximum score you can get is 140. If you get that score or 14 you are lying to yourself.

I suspect that to be a successful as an entrepreneur a score of 8 to 10 in each dimension would make you very likely to succeed. More impotently take a look at which dimensions you score lower than 8 and consider how you can improve that dimension.

If you want to be successful as an entrepreneur then you can always get better.

Today's question is:
"How happy are you with your entrepreneur score?"

Tuesday, August 13, 2013

365QOD- Day920

Post it. They will come.

"From blog to a book."- Fast company article title

Sometimes I marvel at what I read. Often times it justifies something that I thought about few years back. This title is one example of this.

In February of 2011 I started this blog. Almost immediately I stared seeing the potential that this blog could become a book. I thought about it and let it leave my mind.

A year later I did exactly that. The thought became a book. I recently finished volume two of my blog books. Guess what? I am not going to stop. Next year volume three will come out. So the title for this post should be from blog to books.

I do not advertise my blog or my books. People find them organically. That is by design. I make very little money of the books and no money from the blog.

In the last couple of days my third book came out. It is the 365QOD Volume II. The cover is shown below.

Today's question is:
"What could you blog about for 920 days?"

Monday, September 2, 2013

365QOD- Day940

Shift Happens...did you catch it?

"Shift happens- profit from it"-sector rotational journal slogan

What a great slogan! We tend to think of change as bad. If we are a bit more flexible we might even welcome some level of change.

But accepting change is one thing. Benefiting from the change is a whole different level. You have to be aware that the shift, the change, is starting to take place.

Once aware, then plan your strategy. But that is not enough. Up to this point it is all mental. You must now execute your plan while looking for opportunities to improve it. No plan is prefect but believe in yourself enough to get the best result possible.

An example of a shift I am watching is the new smart watch movement. I believe that many sensors will integrate with it. I am looking for shifts which I can exploit.

Today's question is:
"Do you profit from shifts?"

Tuesday, September 3, 2013

365QOD- Day941

I Don't Need It

"The Ph.D. taught me to be a fast learner and to have self discipline. NorthrupGrumman taught me to be a good collaborator and how to settle disputes between competing interests. The sales job, obviously, helped me develop relationship skills. It was a process of building an entrepreneur who not only could start a business but could also run a business long term."- Patrick Mish

I recently read an article in Inc. magazine called **Why I wasted a Perfectly Good Doctorate?** The quote is from the article and to me it paints a different picture.

Patrick might not be using his degree in an engineering firm but the skills that he learned are transferable to his new business. It is not uncommon for engineers to never work in engineering but work in other fields. Why? Because if you can figure out engineering courses you can learn anything else.

The one thing that I believe he did not learn is that life is a learning process. He learned enough from school to succeed as an engineer. He also had to learn the skills needed to be a great salesmen. And lastly learn how to be an entrepreneur. As Patrick in the end realizes, it was a process of becoming an entrepreneur.

I do not think education is a waste if you learn how to learn. If you just get good grades but do not learn how to learn then you are just getting a piece a paper. As Patrick eventually learned, if you learn how to learn you can figure anything out.

Today's question is:
"**Have you learned how to learn?**"

Friday, October 25, 2013

365QOD- Day993

Economy for Stupid

"I want to draw a cat for you. I want to draw a cat for you...."-Steve Gadlin

I watched an old segment of Shark Tank season three in which an entrepreneur came on the show, danced for the investors, and asked them to invest 10k for 25% of his company. He charged about ten dollars to create a drawing and post it on his website so that the person can download it.

When introducing the idea he said, "There is an economy for stupid and I am overflowing with it." I could not resist writing this line down. It made me wonder if he is correct that people want to buy stupid stuff.

If we look back to the seventies we see the pet rock. Paint a cute look on a rock, put it in a cute box and ship it to people. Millions later the entrepreneur is laughing all the way to the bank. Remember the cabbage patch kids? Elmo?

Same types of examples can be found for the eighties, nineties till today. People are interested in buying things that fit the economy of stupid idea. The only question is how do we exploit it and make money?

Today's question is:
"What can you contribute to the economy of stupid and make money?"

Sunday, October 27, 2013

365QOD- Day995

Phone Brick

"A lot of people hate changing their phone"-a news story hook

The other day I watched the evening news and heard a story about a young guy who had come up with a way to change the way we update our phones. His idea was to make the phone modular. The PC is made up of many sub systems. If you want a CD drive you put one in. If you want to add an additional hard drive there is a slot for that. You want to change the video card, take it out and put in a better one.

The story explained his idea by showing that one side of the phone is simply a screen. Behind the screen was a two sided base into which one side plugged in the screen. It plugged in pretty much like a Lego block.

On the other side of the base the user could choose what functions and capabilities were important to them. So you want extra-long battery time, plug in two battery blocks. Don't need Wi-Fi then take the block out. Don't need a sound card take out that block. If you need more memory then add an additional block of memory.

You get the idea. To this phone block you would add or remove blocks to fit your purpose. I think that the idea is very interesting but late. Most of us expect to get a new phone every two years in order to keep up with all of the new changes in capabilities. We want that new shiny toy.
I am not convinced that we want to modify our old toy. Maybe I am wrong? For most of us a phone is a toy, not a tool. The new and shiny appeals to us.

Today's question is:
"Would you stay with your old phone if you could modify it or do you want a new one?"

Tuesday, November 12, 2013

365QOD- Day1011

Unloved Products

"First, find the most annoying, obvious problem that millions of people deal with every day. Then ask if things really have to be that way."- Andy Rooney's business plan according to Farhad Manjoo

While reading a Wall Street Article on **Big Innovations from Small Annoyances** by Farhad Manjoo, I read this line by Tony Fadell, **"There are products that have been unloved, that are basically the same as when we were growing up"**. It immediately pulled me in and got me thinking.

What pulled me in was the unloved products part. By his definition these are products that have not changed since we were little. In other words, what products that function and most likely look the same for the last 30+ years that you use every day?

What product fits this mold? The thermostat that Nest redesigned certainly fits this mold. It took the thermostat and made it cool and sells it at $250.

Any ideas? How about the toaster? The microwave? The can opener? Can these be redesigned to become cool once again? There are many unloved products to which we can apply Andy Rooney's business plan idea and come up with newer and better cooler versions.

Today's question is:

"What is an unloved product that you use every day?"

Wednesday, November 13, 2013

365QOD- Day1012

What is Next

"If all of the wealth is taken away from the 1% within 10 years they would be back in the 1%"- Anonymous

The quote is something that I had heard before and it makes sense to me. If you know how to do something, and if you did not just get lucky, you should be able to recreate your path to success. In theory it should be no harder to do it a second time.

Today I was having a conversation with a friend, Tommy, when this topic came up. He shared his business success story and his eventual failure. However, he has not been able to repeat the success.

As we decomposed his story it quickly became obvious that many years ago he noticed an opportunity. He quickly saw the next step in the opportunity and jumped on it. Next he grew it. According to him, his demise was due to lack of certain management skills.

He pointed out that he has never seen another opportunity like the one he exploited. I quickly reminded him that in his current role he comes across many people that are very successful. All he has to do is ask them.

I suggested that he ask them, **"What opportunity are you excited about now?"** Once, he gets pulled into their world then I suggested for him to ask himself, **"What is next?"** This is in order to allow his brain to explore the next step needed to exploit that opportunity or come up with a new original opportunity that is loosely based on the one given to him.

We both agreed that one thing that has to be true is that a person has to be "present" in the now in order to recognize opportunities. Let yourself be quiet enough to hear and understand the opportunity.

Today's question is:
"What is next in your opportunity?"

Thursday, November 28, 2013

365QOD- Day1027

Power Networking

"INTRODUCE YOURSELF & I'LL GIVE YOU A $1"- Scott Gerber t-shirt slogan

Imagine walking around a networking event with a t-shirt that has this slogan on it. What would you predict would be the outcome? Scott Gerber did it and turned a $62 dollar investment into five clients and thousands of dollars in revenue.

This idea is similar to that of Scott Ginberg I wrote about in Post997. Scott walks around with a name tag with his name on it. He has done it for four years and it has resulted in multiple books. Again, a very successful result.

What these two stories have in common is the ability to pull people in. One does it with money and the other one by letting people know his name. Maybe the rest of us are too guarded and shy?

I believe that these two guys are onto something. Maybe combining them into a single t-shirt with your name on it with the slogan that if people introduce themselves to you, you would pay them $1 is the best. I believe that people are scared of paying one dollar per introduction.

Suppose you went to a function and tested the idea with 100 dollar bills in your pocket and actually doing it. That is the extreme of your loss. Noting that Scott only gave away $62 dollars he most likely spoke to most people 2-5 minutes per person. So 100 singles would give you anywhere from 3 hours and 20 minutes to 8 hours and 20 minutes talk marathon. Consider that his return at minimum was more than 200+ times the investment.

The magic would be to make the 2-5 minutes meaningful for both you and the person that is introducing themselves. You want their info and contact information but you also want to hook them into what you are doing that would resonate with them. If they are willing to continue talking and take action by purchasing your product then the $1 is peanuts if you could get 200+ times the return.

Today's question is:
"Would you pay $1 for an introduction?"

Friday, November 29, 2013

365QOD- Day1028

Anti-Business Plan

"The One Paragraph Start-Up Plan"- section heading in Scott Gerber's book <u>Never Get a Real Job</u>

I am currently reading this book. The first eighty pages were all about what not to do. Even though I agreed with most things I could care less about what not to do. But when I saw this section immediately I started to enjoy the book.

Most business plans are not worth the paper that they are written on. People over predict a rosy picture that is not realistic. But just because someone writes it down it must be important. Some plans are so full of pages that they require a book binding.

Scott suggestion is brilliant. Write a very tight one paragraph business plan. That by itself is brilliant but what I really was impressed with is that he tells you to convert it into an action step and to test it as if it is a hypothesis (belief that could be true or false). He suggests that you test each sentence by doing it and using these eight questions: "
1. What is the service your business performs or the product it provides today?
2. How does your business produce or provide the product or service right now?
3. How will customers use your product or service as it exists right now?
4. How will your business generate immediate revenue?
5. Who are the primary clients your business will target immediately?
6. How will you market your start-up to prospective clients with the resources you have at your direct disposal?
7. How are you different than your competitors right now?
8. What are the secondary and tertiary client bases you will target once you've attains success with your primary base?"

This idea lines up well with the Lean Start-Up idea of producing a minimum product and testing it. Once each step has been completed he suggests that you evaluate your overall findings by asking yourself these six questions:"
1. What worked and what didn't?
2. What was the result of each action step?
3. Was the overall experience positive or negative? Why?
4. What did you learn during the process?
5. Which steps can be modified or improved for better results? How?
6. Which steps need to be deleted all together?"

Pretty cool!

Today's question is:
"Can you narrow your start-up idea to one paragraph <u>and</u> break it apart into actionable steps?"

Saturday, November 30, 2013

365QOD- Day1029

Visualize Your Goals with Storyboards

"Storyboards show you things that words cannot, and they help bridge words to experience"- Joe Gebbia, AinBnB

Write down an idea on a storyboard, envision it, and draw that snapshot moment where the idea enters the world. What is one thing you can do next to move your idea forward?

My answer is storyboard. I am a great believer in storyboards.

- Most of us think visually. 58 percent of all communication is visual.

- 38 percent is tonality.

- Only 7 percent is the actual words we say.

So if we want to communicate to ourselves the best way is through visual means.

Many years ago I thought that creating a storyboard business was a wonderful business idea. I thought of creating a website that would allow one to insert pictures on a storyboard along different themes and then to have the final color version sent to you as a printed poster. This would be cool to create and even cooler to have a poster of the idea.

I might just have to execute this.

Today's question is:
"Have you ever used a storyboard to visualize your future?"

Friday, December 13, 2013

365QOD- Day1042

Happiness App

"When you start monitoring anything, you start learning"- Robert Trajkovski

Nataly Kogan has a company that produces an app called Happier. The app helps users document the things that make them happiest. The eventual goal of the app is to have enough data to be able to generate a happiness graph. Cool!

In past posts I talked about the MyFitnessPal app which allows me to track my daily calories and exercise inputs. I love the app although for the last month or so it has failed to work.

I do not see Nataly's app as being anything different. It allows the user to track their level of activity along a certain dimension. She tracks happiness, MyFitnessPal tracks calorie and activity level.

What these two apps are telling me is that people want to track themselves and the easier you can make it for them to convert their lives into data the more financially rewarding it will be for your business.

Today's question is:

"What would you track in your life that can be graphed?"

Friday, December 20, 2013

365QOD- Day1049

Remote Controlled Paper Airplane

"For how long will it hold their interest?" -my first thought

The other day was flipping through a bunch of stories online and one stopped me to think. It was a story about how a group has gotten funding through Kickstarter for a device that could be attached to a paper airplane to help improve the flight time. The device is controlled from a smart phone.

This story kept coming back up in my mind. Most of us when we were little played with paper planes. And in the end we never quite got great at making them, we moved on to different toys. Do kids these days even build paper airplanes?

The power of the idea is in making something old into something new by adding technology to make it cool. I believe that if you had a controllable paper plane in a park you would be swarmed by kids wanting to give it a try. They would put their phones and iPads down to be able to control a physical object through the phone. I do not think that paper would matter to them. As a matter of fact after a while they would want one made up of special materials that they can fly with more control.

Today's question is:

"What old game you played can be turned into a cool new toy?"

Sunday, January 19, 2014

365QOD- Day1079

The Spark of Invention

"Summer 1995...I wanted to invest in an IPO for gaming company. The company went public at $15 a share. My broker calls me and says, 'Well, you got the stock at $24. ' I'm like, ' How come?' He said, 'Well, $15 was the ideal price, not the price that people like you can get.' I was like, 'What do you mean people like me?' The takeaway was that the theory of efficient markets is really great- in theory. In practice, regular people are locked out.

I started thinking. This internet thing- maybe I could use it to help people bring power of financial markets to regular people. Of course, regular people aren't selling stocks in their households. They're selling stuff. I thought there's a real opportunity to create a marketplace that could bring the power of efficient markets to regular people. So that's what I did that Labor Day in 1995."- Pierre Omidyar, E-Bay founder

Pierre started Ebay in order to solve a problem. He felt the problem when he could not purchase a good at the price that was advertised. He then realized that this problem exists for all of us. Lastly, he realized that the opportunity for many folks was different than what he was trying to take advantage off. This process is the spark.

Unfortunately, most of us do not think that way. If we have a problem we most often just get mad and complain. We might think of a solution to that specific problem. And that is where it ends.

The difference is that we don't always look for the need. Pierre realized that the need was in a completely different arena. By understanding the pain he and others felt and then transferring that pain into a solution to the need he succeeded.

Today's question is:
"Can you transfer the pain into the spark?"

Wednesday, January 29, 2014

365QOD- Day1088

The Seven Year Plan

"I don't know why the word "lazy" gets such a bad rap -- I'm a big fan of lazy."- Brenton Hayden

Brenton Hayden wrote an article in Entrepreneur magazine about how he constructed a plan when he was 21 to retire at 27. A seven year plan. The quote is the start of his article.

After reading the article I noticed that he did not explain his starting point too well. He mentioned that at 21 he had a business that was a year old. The article does not explain how much he needed to start the business, where the money came from, and his financial position.

But he does do a great job explaining that he came up with a plan to retire at 27 and that he had to create a business that would be self-sustaining without him. While reading the article I could not help but note the similarities to the strategy I read in the book **Build to Sell**. I take my hat off to him that he pulled it off.

I am impressed with Benton. He created a seven year exit plan and executed it. I wish all of us were better at creating and executing our plans. But it is never too late to create and execute. The execution of such a plan has nothing to do with the financial end. It has everything to do with having the freedom to do anything that you wish to do for the rest of your life without financial worries. That is a true freedom.

By the way, I would definitely not classify him as lazy.

Today's question is:

"Do you have a seven year exit plan?"

Exceeding

Sunday, March 17, 2013

365QOD- Day771

"Here's what's in our DNA at Apple. We stand at the intersection of art and science; at the intersection of creativity and technology"- Steve Jobs

Imagine four intersecting circles.
> Top left is Art (A).
> Top right is Creativity(C).
> Bottom left is Technology (T).
> Bottom right is Science(S).

Apple owns the ACTS intersection.

I believe that this idea should be the playbook for any company that wants to succeed. If a company can create products that fit that intersection then it will survive and thrive.

Unfortunately many well-known companies will survive by being in three out of four circles. Microsoft is a great example. They do not make anything that fits the Art circle. Their products are functional but not fun.

In my opinion, recently Samsung has been developing into a company that is joining Apple in the ACTS area. In other words it is possible to push one's company into the intersection.

Today's question is:
"Could you develop something that fits in the ACTS intersection?"

Sunday, February 2, 2014

365QOD- Day1092-91

Correcting an Expert

"I can see at least 2 mistakes in his form."- My thought

Yesterday I was in a book store. I did an usual thing. While looking through the magazine section I picked up a martial arts magazine. Usually I pick up business and success magazines.

In the magazine were many great stories about techniques and people. One made me take a second look. In the story it showcased the skill set of a grandmaster. It caught my interest.

I paused and took a look at some of the pictures. In one of the pictures, the grand-master was shows doing a step in the most basic white belt form. I kept looking at it and immediately saw several mistakes. The left hand was striking the wrong target because of the angle. Similarly, the right hand was not cocked and ready for the next strike. His footwork was also poor. The positioning was such that he had very poor balance.

Am I picky? Who do I think I am? A grandmaster?

The point of this story is that if we look closely at the work of others it is very easy to poke holes. We do not even have to be a grandmaster to spot the mistakes. We just have to be open to learning and noticing.

It is easy to throw stones at others. The bigger question is whether I am aware of my own hand and foot positioning when I do the form or do I just sloppily perform the most basic form?

Today's question is:
"Can you be truly critical of your own work?"

Fear

Tuesday, April 2, 2013

365QOD- Day787

"Fear is a liar" - words on a wall

A couple of weeks ago I offered this quote to Maria, my co-worker. This morning she came back at me with her own version, "**Fear is expensive**".

Wow! I love her version. It made me think how it is so true. Fearing can reduce the number of opportunities that we pursue and ultimately it costs us potential income.

Today's question is:
"What else is fear?"

Tuesday, April 16, 2013

365QOD- Day 801

"I would rather have a life full of 'oh wells' rather than a life full of 'what ifs'"- unknown

I was looking through a few hundred photos that I recently downloaded and came across this quote. It immediately got me to think.

I believe that most of us tend to live lives full of what ifs with some oh wells. I do not think that it is all or nothing.

The secret is to switch the two. Live a life with mostly oh wells and almost no what ifs. How? By confronting every fear that we have until the fog of fear is eliminated. In the end, by facing them we become more fulfilled.

Today's question is:
"What oh well will you face today?"

Friday, June 7, 2013

365QOD- Day854

"That scares me to death." -often heard

When I was young I was afraid of heights. Anything above ground was too high. If I had to stand on a balcony I felt my legs full of fear. I could not lean over.

Over time I have managed to overcome this fear. Now I can comfortably sit and lean over the edge on a balcony and never fear it.

At work I can climb large structures and never feel scared. How did I overcome the fear? I believe that just getting older and realizing that it is an unfounded fear. Maybe exposing myself to heights? I have never jumped from a plane or bungee jumped but I believe I could do it.

My last fear is snakes. I have never held a snake without fear. Maybe I need to overcome it?

Today's question is:
" What is a current fear that you have?"

Sunday, July 7, 2013

365QOD- Day884

"Fearcast"- new word

I was listening to an audio book on happiness when I heard this word. It is a word that combines the words fear and forecast into a single word.

Since the first part is fear, the word emphasizes fear. It made me wonder how often our future forecasts are based on fear. If they are, then we are setting ourselves us for failure.

Why? In my opinion when you focus on fear then you are wasting energy towards that instead focusing it on the solution. As Henry Ford said,
"If you think you can or if you think you can't, you are right."
My version is,
"If you fear it, or you fear it not, you are right."

Today's question is:
"Do you focus on the fear or on the solution?"

Wednesday, October 9, 2013

365QOD- Day977

Scared of What

"Give no mercy to your FEARS."- Anonymous

Long time ago I read somewhere that we can look at most of our decisions and note why we made them. How? Imagine a circle with a line inside it splitting it in half vertically. Write the word faith in the left semicircle. Inside the right semicircle write the word fear.

Faith is a belief that you can on your own or that you will through some external help from another person or God prevail. There is no doubt about the end result. So you move towards it.

The fear side is more complicated. It is the belief that you cannot on your own nor with the help of another person or God prevail. But more than a belief, you are held into place or pushed back by an invincible force that you will not even try it. That is the force of fear.

As the quote advises, give no mercy to your fears. Once they have an inch they will demand a yard. Push back and say that despite your fear you will push forward. As Churchill wisely advised, **"Never. Never. Never ever give up. Never."** Push forward.

Today's question is:
"Is your belief on an issue based on faith or fear?"

Feelings

Sunday, March 3, 2013

365QOD-Day757

"I got it!"- Maria Gonzalez

Maria and I had a conversation about perfumes a couple of weeks ago. I mentioned to her that I tend to notice a nice perfume smell on people and often will complement the person. I also told her that even though I put on a different scent each day, I never get complimented. Out loud I wondered why.

The other day, she walked in my office and said, "I got it". It bothered her enough to keep thinking about our conversation and come up with an opinion. In her opinion it has to do with sexual harassment Maria believes that because of it, people just keep those compliments to themselves. It is no longer PC to compliment.

This bothers me. I wondered how complimenting a woman or a man that the scent they are using smells good can be misconstrued as harassment. In my world it is a genuine compliment. BUT I guess the rest of the world considers it differently. Which makes me wonder...

Today's question is:
"How do you compliment someone without them feeling harassed?"

Financial

Saturday, February 23, 2013

365QOD- Day749

"I don't give out my salary information. My boss and I are both ashamed of it"- Don Amerson

Recently Don said this to me in a hallway conversation. Man, I could hardly wait to get back to my office to write it down. It is a jewel and great advice.

In Europe where I grew up people telling you their salary is very common. I do not know if it is just not thought of as private or maybe we in the US consider it too private?

I usually do not share that information. It serves no purpose to share it. If I am interviewing for a job then I should be judged based on what I bring to the table NOT based on what I settled for in my last role.

I do believe people see you differently once you give out that information. Some will look up to you and some will look down on you. There is no good that can come from it.

Today's question is:
"What private information do you give out freely?"

Thursday, April 4, 2013

365QOD- Day789

"We asked everyday people to share with us the age of the oldest person they've known by placing a sticker on or chart" - Prudential ad

When I saw this ad on TV I was quickly pulled in. The as displays a large canvas on which people place dots. It quickly demonstrates that we all know someone who has lived in the 80-100 age group.

The ad asks two questions as to why we are living longer but yet the retirement age has not changed and whether we will have enough.

Retirement requires long term planning. Our society trends to reward short term thinking. I believe that we must do both well in order to be successful. Some of my earlier posts offer formulas for you to check your level of readiness to retire.

Today's question is:
"Will you have enough resources to retire well"

Thursday, May 9, 2013

365QOD- Day825

"I am working full time on my job, and I am working part time on my fortune"-Jim Rohn

I love this line. It fits well with my AND thinking belief.

Many people believe that they can only work on something full time. But then they miss out on working on their fortune part. Both are important.

It is so easy to just come up with reasons. Reasons such as lack of time, money, too busy, etc. come to mind very quickly.

It all boils down to what is important to you: working for yourself or for someone else.

Today's question is:
" Are you working on your or someone else's fortune?"

Sunday, July 14, 2013

365QOD- Day891

"Don't fill your ego, fill your bank account"-James Malichak

I believe that for most of us money is the great motivator. Without it, I doubt that many of us would show up for work. But this quote addresses a different need.

I believe that working for a living fills a survival need. It is a physical need. We no longer have to hunt to put food on our table or purchase clothing so work is the way we fill these needs.

The need to feed the ego is different. You want to do something because it makes you feel important. You do something not for a true need but to feed the ego.

To me the ultimate test is whether something puts money in my pocket. If it does not, then it must feed the ego. As an example, if I write books and they do not sell then I am feeding the ego. If I write a blog and no one reads it then I am doing it for my ego.

Today's question is:
"Are you feeding your ego or filling your bank account?"

Friday, August 30, 2013

365QOD- Day937

Not my Job

"All kids are born geniuses, none are born financially astute. It is your job as a parent to teach them."- Ron Wheeler

Most parents if given a choice of having a child that is a genius vs. the child that grows up to be a successful adult will choose the later. The skill set is very different and we stay adults for a longer period of time.

Ron's words give one of the dimensions of success as an adult: financially astute. But the problem is that most people will label themselves financially ignorant. Ignorant does not mean stupid. It simply means uneducated in those matters.

So how do you teach them if you are ignorant? Well the best way is together. Create a profit and loss statement for your family. What comes in and what goes out. Then start talking about saving and lastly investing. It might actually be fun to learn it together.

Today's question is:
"Do you keep your genius children ignorant about financial maters?"

Saturday, December 14, 2013

365QOD- Day1043

Listening ROI

"Action-oriented people—like most entrepreneurs—tend to talk more than they listen; I confess I used to be one of them. However, I've found out that speaking burns more energy than listening, and the ROI is generally lower."- Esteban Reyes, Best Advice I ever Got Inc. Magazine article

For non-financial folks the definition for ROI is return on investment. Most of us would never connect listening with return on investment. I know that I do.

As Esteban warns, most of us "entrepreneurial" types tend to talk more than we listen. In my world that is OK but you have to be wise enough to know when to stop. That is the key.

I once negotiated with a company to do some training. During the negotiations the contact asked me what I wanted for a rate. Being new to the business I had a figure in mind. BUT as Esteban cautions, I kept quiet. The contact made the first offer and it was four times higher than what I expected. So I said, "Hum." I then asked to be paid for the development time. She said OK.

The moral of the story is that by keeping quiet I made four times what I expected and got paid to sit in my pajamas to develop the training. Sweet! The ROI was significant because I managed to sense that I would be better off keeping quiet and listening to the offer.

Today's question is:

"How do you know when to listen more than you talk?"

Thursday, December 19, 2013

365QOD- Day1048

Your Relationship with Time

"Work Like a Millionaire - Rich people treat time differently. They buy it, while poor people sell it. The wealthy know time is more valuable than money itself, so they hire people for things they're not good at or aren't a productive use of their time, such as household chores. But don't kid yourself that those who hit it big don't work hard. Financially successful people are consumed by their hunt for success and work to the point that they feel they are winning and not just working."- entrepreneur magazine story

Let us take this quote apart.

The first line that caught my interest us that the wealthy buy time while the rest of us sell it. True! Unless you have residual income coming in from something you have created before you are trading time for money. The only difference is what the value of your hour vs. mine.

Second idea that stands out is that they are willing to hire people for chores that are not productive use of their time. If the time used is nonproductive then choose someone that can productively do it inexpensively. The decision is actually very simple.

Suppose you make 20 dollars an hour and a task will take you three hours to do. The task cost to you is 60 dollars. Now suppose someone is willing to do the task for five dollars an hour and it only takes them two hours to do the work. Your cost is ten dollars and you save fifty dollars. The important gain is more than money. You get three hours to produce at least sixty dollars' worth of product while spending ten dollars to get the task you do not want to do that only costs you ten dollars.

The third idea is the hunt for success. You are hungry to find success while you have released others to do something that they are great at. You need to focus on your path and let others find theirs. This leads to a feeling of winning.

Today's question is:
"Are you winning or losing?"

Focus

Tuesday, May 7, 2013

365QOD- Day823

"There is a business concept called opportunity cost. When you choose one course of action, you miss out on all the other opportunities you might have chosen to pursue but didn't. People rarely stop to consider that until it's too late."- Steve Tobak Inc. magazine

This morning I spent some time thinking about how wasteful my weekend was in total. Yes I got a few things done but no major items got ticked of my list.

This quote teaches a wonderful lesson. I did not consider the opportunity cost of doing the things I chose vs. the big items I could have accomplished. Maybe the value of the NBA game should have been lower than finishing the editing of my new book?

The realization for me is to periodically stop and ask myself as to what is my opportunity cost for choosing to do what I am doing instead of getting an important task done.

Today's question is:
" **How do you establish your opportunity cost of an activity?**"

Wednesday, September 4, 2013

365QOD- Day942

Start Small

"Self control is not genetic or fixed, but rather a skill one can develop and improve with practice."- Roy Baumeister

Our lives tend to be very chaotic. Because of this, we require a significant amount of self-control to work and thrive in this type of environment. Instead of worrying about negative distractions we should focus on activities that are our intended goal.

But how do we build our focus?

Baumeister suggests that we start small. Add a new small habit. Examples of small tasks are improving your posture, saying yes instead of yeah, or flossing your teeth before going to bed. These small tasks seem silly but after a while they become ingrained habits that can be done without requiring thoughts. Once this happens then you can start on another challenge.

Today's question is
"How do you build a small unrelated habit?"

Monday, September 23, 2013

365QOD- Day961

Getting Out of a Funk

"Time spent without purpose is easily forgotten"- Robert Trajkovski

While on vacation the other day I stated moping around. Everything seemed to bother me and I had no peace. I was on vacation and not feeling great or relaxing. I was in a funky mood.

I quickly realized what was missing. I needed a creative endeavor to fill my mind. So I sat down and created 52 small eBooks. Yes, you read that correct, 52 small eBooks.

In the last two years I have written two books based on my blog posts. At the end of the year I take the posts, organize them by topic, and heavily edit them into a book. So this process is one of reorganizing by topic.

My friend Naren, during a walk, suggested that there are many products that can be extracted from my work. I quickly realized that each topic could be an eBook of its own. That is what I did. I took the last two books, combined them, and extracted each topic into a new word file.

The work took me two and a half hours. It was so pleasurable that I immediately felt great. All I needed was a little creative time to get me out of my funk.

Today's question is:
"How do you get out of a funk?"

Sunday, September 29, 2013

365QOD- Day967

Losing Focus

"I got to focus and study."-my words to myself

I have spent the last month or so studying for a PMP exam. This is a Project Management Professional certification.

I am struggling to keep my focus on the end goal. It has been years since I took a class and had to pass a test. Years!

I realized a few months ago that I need to increase my formal learning. Since I made that realization, I have taken two courses: green belt six sigma and a PMP prep course.

So why am I having a hard time focusing and studying? There are many things going through my mind that are life and work related. It is as simple as that. I need to clear my mind plate before I can focus. Probably the best way is to sit down with a piece of paper and do a brain dump. Get it down and then I can move on.

Today's question is:
"How do you know when you are losing your focus?"

Tuesday, October 1, 2013

365QOD- Day969

What are you chasing?

"If money is your hope for independence you will never have it. The only real security that a man will have in this world is a reserve of knowledge, experience, and ability."-Henry Ford

I am chasing financial freedom. What this means to me is being able to stop having to go to work every day and work on my creative projects full time while earning more than I earn now. According to Mr. Ford, the road has three requirements.

I need to have the knowledge (K) to create the products that the world needs. This knowledge could be how to write, how to edit, how to market, how to sell, etc.

Second requirement is experience (E). I still do not have marketing experience. I can produce my products but I have no clue on marketing the products to mass audience. Selling is also a weak spot. I have improved my writing and editing.

The third piece is ability (A). Just because I know what to do, experience doing it in the past, I still need ability to do the work at an exceptional level. Some could be God given and most needs to be developed.

Today's question is:
"Do you see how KEA plays a role in your independence?"

Friday, January 3, 2014

365QOD- Day1063

The Year of the Sales

"You want to be the best-writing author and I am the best-selling author"- paraphrase of Robert Kiyosaki advice to an interviewer

I have written three books in the last three years. My sales have been weak. Is it because the books are just not good? I do not believe that is the case. I think it is about marketing to the right audience.

Books are no different that websites or products. If you have the best product but no one knows about you or have seen your product then you should not be surprised that the product does not move. You have a better mousetrap but people are not aware of it.

Every year I like to create a theme to help me focus for the year. Last year I titled my year **The Year of the App.** My goal was to create an app. I produced my Business Academy app and placed it in the Google Market for free. It was my test run on what it took to make an app and put it out on the market. The intent was not to make money but to understand the process and to be able to use this source for income generation if needed.

The theme for this year is **The Year of the Sales.** I want to market my products and see if I can nudge the sales up. It is my goal to understand how to market in social media and re-package my products so that I can attract many customers and readers. I want to drive myself to best-selling status. So how will I know I am successful? If the sales amount to 25% of my income I would judge my experiment successful.

Today's question is:

"What is this the year of _____ for you?"

Giving

Sunday, February 17, 2013

365QOD- Day743

"'If there is a God, how can he allow this to happen? How can he let so many people suffer?'

Several years ago, I married a man of strong faith. One day he sent an email to
me that said this: 'On a street corner I saw a cold, shivering girl in a thin dress,
with no hope of a decent meal. I got angry and said to God, 'Why did you permit this? Why don't you do something about it?' God
replied, 'I certainly did something about it. I made you.'"- Lisa Ling
Give of Yourself advice

I remember reading this portion in a book and it immediately made me think how we want God to take care of all of our problems. Is that fair to us?

Yes, you read that. If we give away that power then we are powerless to help each other. As the story illustrates then why does God need us? He created us to do what?

We are the tool for most of his miracles. Our purpose here is to help one another. God is there to cover the big stuff.

Today's question is:
"What small miracle did you help God with today?"

Grit

Saturday, April 13, 2013

365QOD- Day798

"A true measure of your life is how much you would be worth if you lost everything"- Robert Trajkovski

I read a quote today which stated that a true measure of your wealth is what you would be worth if you lost everything. It seemed to me that it was missing something.

Wealth is but one dimension on which to measure life. Recently I worked on a workbook of 26 power virtues that one would evaluate along physical, emotional, mental, spiritual, interpersonal, and financial dimensions.

Wealth is simply the financial dimension. I thought of a complete loss of everything: wealth, family, career, friends, etc. would be more drastic.

Where would you begin to rebuild? Would you have the courage to even start? This is kind of a dark chain of thoughts. In the end I concluded that any loss in a singular dimension should not stop you for too long, unless you let it.

Today's question is:
"**Where would you begin the rebuilding process after a devastating loss in any one of the six dimensions?**"

Saturday, January 11, 2014

365QOD- Day1071

The Taste of Pain

"Recycle your pain"- Eric Thomas

The other day I listened to several YouTube segments in which Eric motivates people to not use excuses to live a meaningful life. The videos are pretty motivating messages that take excuses off the table.

This line appeared on one of the screen shots and immediately I knew that I had to comment on it. What does pain taste like?

I believe that we often get motivated or de-motivated by people and events. Unfortunately, most often it is the demotivating that tends to stick with us. Just because someone tells us that we cannot do something, we allow it to become our reality. It does not have to be BUT we just accept it.

This line teaches us to taste the pain of being demoralized and to recycle it to better use. The taste should motivate us to move forward and achieve. In many classic Bruce Lee fight scenes he tastes his own blood that someone has caused and gets motivated to kick their tail.

Paint should be the source of wanting to do better. For most of us it takes a mind shift before we can recycle the pain for benefit. But we must be like Bruce. Taste it and use it against the causer.

Today's question is:

"Do you recycle your pain for good cause?"

Happiness

Thursday, February 7, 2013

365QOD- Day733

"Do you want me to smile on a Monday?" – Actual question posed to me

My answer is no. I cannot make you do anything. You are an adult and have control of yourself. If you do not want to smile then you will not.

I believe that Mondays are critical to team effectiveness. I put on my best smiley face on Mondays. Why?

Spring of 1993 I suffered four major setbacks that each occurred on a Monday. I was responsible for several shops and all of the equipment in them. On Monday morning I would show up for work before 7 and the technicians would tell me how they needed my help to troubleshoot a machine that they had been working on all weekend. I would spend the day working with them and at the end of the day the machine was still not fixed.

Demoralized by not fixing it, I went home to open my mail and discovered that I had been rejected from another Ph.D. program. I would then shower and get ready to go teach my first engineering class.

After this had happened for four weeks in a row, I remember lecturing in front of 75 people and one of the students, David Zajakala, asking me if I was all right. He pointed out that I am not the same guy that started the class. It dawned on me that I had let these Monday experiences affect my teaching.

It was that night that I made a wow to myself to never have a bad Monday. I realized that it affected not only me but other people around me.

I chose to be positive, especially on Mondays. I believe that positivity on Monday also affects the rests of the week.

Today's question is:
"How do you begin your Mondays?"

Wednesday, July 17, 2013

365QOD- Day893

"A man once told Buddha, 'I Want Happiness.' Buddha replied, ' First, remove the 'I'; that is ego. Then remove the 'Want'; that is desire. And now all you're left with is Happiness'" - wisdom

I read this quote this morning and immediately saw the wisdom. We often want things without knowing the reason.

By parsing the sentence, the teacher illustrates that the true need is buried deep in the request. Once the ego is removed you see the action 'want happiness.' Then when one removes the desire the action is no longer needed. What we are left with is the true need: Happiness. This is a need that can be fulfilled simply by being.

Rewrite the story with 'I want a new watch' and remove the ego and desire and all that is left is new watch. But is it the watch or the ability to tell time that is the true need? If it is the watch then it is most likely not a need but a fashion want. If it is the ability to tell time then a phone or an inexpensive watch will fulfill the need.

In the end, the two stories teach us to make sure to strip away everything but the true need.

Today's question is:
"How do you determine a true need? "

Saturday, December 28, 2013

365QOD- Day1057

A Formula For Happiness

"Most folks are as happy as they make up their minds to be."- Abraham Lincoln

God bless the PBS funding drives. It is during these drives that I always get to see unusual programs that I never seem to see the rest of the year. This was also true the other day when I caught a portion of Deepak Chopra's happiness seminar.

I did not see most of it but one slide he presented was full of wisdom. With the slide he presented a formula for happiness. It was made up three pieces.

The first piece is **SetPoint in the Brain**. According to Deepak, our brain's own happiness set point makes up anywhere from **40-50%** of our overall happiness level. In other words, our own internal belief of how happy we are makes up almost half of our actual level of happiness. The old saying, "misery loves company" should become, "Happiness leads to more happiness." Lincoln's quote specifically identifies this set point as the key to happiness.

The second piece is **Conditions of Living**. He believes that it contributes **7-12%** towards our level of happiness. If you are struggling to meet ends meet then this places a burden on your mind and leads to less happiness. So put your financial, work, and home life in order and your happiness score goes up by 10%.

Last piece that makes up happiness is **Voluntary Choices**. Deepak believes that this part contributes **40-50%** towards our happiness level. So if we make bad choices we cannot expect good results. If we make good choices we cannot guarantee good results BUT they become more likely to lead to our happiness level improving.

All together the formula is
Happiness= SetPoint in the Brain + Conditions of Living + Voluntary Choices

What is interesting about this formula is, that when you pull back and examine the three pieces; we are in charge of all three pieces. We can set our happiness set point higher by exposing ourselves to positive inputs continuously. Slowly we can change our living conditions to be better by attacking each area of our lives and nudging it to a better state. In the end we cannot expect overnight to reach nirvana overnight but choice by choice we can improve our choices and the level of happiness.

Today's question is:
"How happy are you based on your set point, conditions, and choices?"

Influence

Wednesday, March 13, 2013

365QOD- Day767

"Do not be an email queen."- Squire Elliot

I worked with Squire for about a year. When I first joined my current company he gave me this advice. This advice was due to a former member of our team just staying in his office and sending emails out to people.

He told me that once I sent an email to follow it up with a visit to the person. In his observations he noted that people quickly forgot about an email but tended to remember the visit and the request.

I have followed Mr. Squire Elliot's advice and it has made a great deal of difference in my experience at work. Connecting in person makes a big deal to most people who are overwhelmed with the flood of email requests.

Today's question is:
"Do you connect in person?

Monday, March 18, 2013

365QOD- Day772

"Never be bullied into silence. Never allow yourself to be made a victim. Accept no one's definition of your life. Define yourself"- Anonymous

I recently saw this quote. Often we are bullied into silence. We give away our power and play the victim card. Fear? I believe that is one part BUT that we also allow others to define our life.

In the end the only way to succeed is to define yourself. Destroy your limits. Define your dreams. Find your voice and be the victor. Others will push you but you have to allow them to move you.

Today's question is:
"How do you define yourself?"

Wednesday, December 11, 2013

365QOD- Day1040

How Do You Judge a Book?

"Not that many"- My words after reading Malcolm Gladwell's David and Goliath book

In my opinion, one way I judge a book is by the number of pages I have dog eared. This allows me to quickly go back through the book and re-read the key points. Oftentimes some of these marked pages become topics for a future blog post.

Why is this important? Well, I thought that this is a good way to judge a book. But maybe I am wrong? I just got through Malcolm's book and only made four marks. I enjoyed most of the book and was excited to tell others to pick up the book before I finished?

The book is very interesting but not very useful to me as a thinking tool. This could be because, even though I enjoyed it, I had issues with some of the conclusions. But I never expect to find a book that I completely agree with. So it is because of the lack of new thoughts that I only noted four pages.

Today's question is:
"How do you judge a book?"

Wednesday, January 15, 2014

365QOD- Day1075

Positive vs. Negative Influencers

"Simply put, you want to deliberately reduce and restrict the amount of your time left vulnerable to random thought or association, and deliberately, sharply reduce the amount of time given to association with people who won't make any productive contribution and may do harm. Does that mean you can only spend time with people you are in complete philosophical agreement with? No. In fact, such isolationism can be dangerous. But it does mean you should avoid association with people who believe and promulgate beliefs diametrically opposed to "success orientation."- Dan Kennedy

You want to deliberately increase the amount of your time directed at chosen thinking and input, and constructive, productive association. You time should be spent with strivers and achievers, with winners and champions. These types of people become an uplifting force that translates into peak performance. In the end being this deliberate makes all your time more valuable.

Is this hard to do? I believe anything is achievable if you nudge yourself towards that goal a little at a time. Spend some time classifying the people in your life as positive or negative force. Then repeat this exercise at least every six months.

Today's question is:

"Have you ever classified the people in your life as positive or negative influencers?"

Leadership

Wednesday, February 6, 2013

365QOD- Day732

"Not my problem"- Unknown

If you want to control something then you have to take ownership. Just because someone else provides the vision, you have to own the process in order to execute it properly. You can't be the owner without control. Giving someone responsibility without authority never works.

I have never gotten push back when I took ownership of a process. It seems to me that most people want to be participants rather than owners. Owners are not necessarily the "owner" of the company. It could be an owner of a process, location, tools, etc.

As owner you do not have a person you can blame. Tag, you are it. You own it and want it to succeed. So you must nurture it to success even when you see your baby failing. It is not easy.

The good side of ownership is that you can be given credit for its success.

Today's question is:
"Do you want the responsibility of ownership?"

Sunday, December 15, 2013

365QOD- Day1044

Legitimate Authority- Part 1

"When people in authority want the rest of us to behave, it matters- first and foremost- how they behave."- Malcolm Gladwell

In next three posts I want to explore these principles of legitimacy. So let us begin with the first principle.

Principle#1: People who are followers have to feel like they have a voice. If they speak up that they will be heard.

Oftentimes leaders will take a look at the unit they are responsible for and would like to make a change. Sometimes the change is market driven and often times it is a performance improvement driven. So the leader wants to or is instructed to make the change.

This principle teaches us that just because you as the leader want to make the change it still needs to be communicated to your followers. And even better, when your followers make a suggestion or challenge your change effort to take that feedback to modify and improve the change effort.

Without that push back and feedback you are only as good as your desire to change. By using the feedback you get stronger and the change is more likely to be accepted and followed.

Today's question is:

"How do you make sure that your followers have their voices heard?"

Monday, December 16, 2013

365QOD- Day1045

Legitimate Authority- Part 2

Principle#2 A leader has to set up a system that is predictable. There has to be a reasonable expectation that the rules that we will follow tomorrow are going to be roughly the same as the rules today.

One way to think through this is to realize that if A leads to B then tomorrow A+ (a slightly changed A) must lead to B+ (slightly different output B). If A does not lead to C then tomorrow A+ should not lead to C+. In other words, I cannot tell you something different tomorrow than today and for you not to lose my trust. I have to be predictable in order to be considered legitimate.

I have seen leaders who announce a change one week and next week go against the change that they announced. This causes confusion and lack of trust because the team will wonder what the following week will bring.

Everyone has a change level and if you make the change too steep, many followers will get lost.

Today's question is:

"How predictable are your small changes?"

Tuesday, December 17, 2013

365QOD- Day1046

Legitimate Authority- Part 3

Principle#3 When one is in authority position, they are expected to be fair. They have to treat each member in the group equally. Discipline cannot be enforced when one has their favorites.

Many years ago I was managing a large team. One of the employees did something that was not allowed. Instead of having his immediate supervisor write him up I wrote him up. Why?

Joe was a very popular guy. Everyone loved Joe. He had not intentionally violated the policy but he did violate it. So as the manager I wrote him up. When I was confronted by other employees as to why I wrote him up my answer was in order to be able to write them up. They were puzzled.

If I did not write Joe, who everyone loved, then I would not be fair when I wrote someone else for the same offense. You have to treat your followers as equals. As a person you might get along with someone better than another but they are still your followers and deserve to be treated as equals.

Today's question is:

"Do you have favorites or do you play fair?"

Wednesday, January 1, 2014

365QOD- Day1061

Real Leaders

"Wannabes are something like metric-maximizing robots. Given a set of numbers they must 'hit,' they beaver away trying to hit them. The leader knows their job is very different: not merely to maximize existing metrics, which are often part of the problem (hi, GDP, shareholder value), but to re-imagine them. The leader's job is, fundamentally, not merely to 'hit a target'- but to redesign the playing field. It's architecture, not mere archery. If you're hitting a target, you are not a leader. You're just another performer, in an increasingly meaningless game."- Umair Haque

This is a powerful quote. It helps differentiate between goal hitting and 're-designing the field'. Targets could be given to you and might not be correct. They are often opinions of what detached leaders of leaders believe it is going on. They have a good view of external factors BUT when it comes down to specific targets typically they are fuzzy.

As a front line leader you must 're-imagine' the metrics to make them meaningful and actionable. If they are not achievable you are setting your team up for failure. It is your job to help them feel that they can succeed with your help.

I think that meaningful targets could pull a team forward BUT targets for targets sake are just a game and have no meaning. The targets are best derived from bottom up once the vision is shared with the team.

Today's question is:
"Do you re-imagine AND re-design targets that are given to you?"

Learning

Wednesday, April 17, 2013

365QOD- Day802

"How do I explain it to you?" - My question

Recently a gentlemen walked in my office and asked me to explain the capital project flow. So I started explaining it from start to end.

He said that he wanted to learn it from end to start. The process consists of over 25 steps. This exchange made me think. I was presenting the ideal process to him. He was interested in understanding the real process flow with all of the problems along the steps.

I believe that in order to understand a process I tend to want to understand the ideal flow. This takes away the noise of reality. But once the ideal has been learned then the real flow can be studied and optimized.

Today's question is:
"Would you prefer to learn the ideal or real flow of a system?"

Sunday, April 28, 2013

365QOD- Day813

"Can't teach an old dog new tricks." - Outdated wisdom

This morning I read the April issue of Men's Health. In it I found an article about Mark Peterson.

Mark Peterson is a professor at University of Michigan. His areas of focus are physical medicine and rehabilitation. What made the story interesting is that even though he had a PhD he is working on a Masters in clinical research.

To me this is impressive. Here is a guy who can easily rest on his education but instead he has decided to close a gap. I believe that in the future Mark's reality will be everyone reality. We will spend most of our lives learning new tricks. Without these new tricks we will limit ourselves and future opportunities.

Today's question is:
" **How do you learn new tricks?**"

Monday, April 29, 2013

365QOD- Day814

"I am the old dog" - my thought

Today begins the second week of lean six sigma green belt training course. I am loving every minute of the training.

Around year 2000 I was a mid-level Engineering Manager in a steel mill. Six sigma was being introduced in the steel industry and I was asked if I wanted to become a black belt. I turned it down because I did not expect to be there very long.

Turning down the training was a mistake. I have regretted that choice twice in my life. Recently my company offered the training and my team and I decided to take advantage of it. It is another problem solving tool in our toolbox.

Today's question is:
"Have you ever turned down training and lived to regret it?"

Tuesday, May 28, 2013

365QOD- Day844

"To 'know thyself' is hard work. Harder still is to believe that you, with all of your flaws, are enough- without checking in, tweeting an update, or sharing a photo a proof of your existence for the approval of your 791 followers. A healthy relationship with your devices is all about taking ownership of your time and making an investment in your life. I'm not calling for any radical, Neo-Luddite movement here. Carving out time for yourself is as easy as doing one thing. Walk your dog. Stroll your baby. Go on a date- without your handheld holding your hand." - James Victore

I love the line know thyself. I have laid out a detailed outline of my autobiography so far. It is intended for my kids to read and one day understand why I have made most of the choices in my life.

The second reason for writing a book like that is to spend some time and truthfully examine myself and the choices I have made. Maybe by knowing myself, I could make better choices in the future.

Today's question is:
"Do you know thyself?"

Saturday, June 8, 2013

365QOD- Day855

"We are sitting here - one is reading your book, the other one is reading your blog" - text response

Yesterday I sent a text to my kids, Stefani and Milan, to see what they were doing. What came back was the above response.

It made my century. As a parent the only thing I wish for is for them to become great people. To be the kind of people others want to be like. In the end to be the best Stefani and the best Milan they can become.

For my children to read my book and my blog tells me that they are still willing to learn. Even greater is that they are willing to learn from me. It inspires me to do better myself.

THANKS Stefani and Milan. Stay teachable.

Today's question is:
"Who inspires you?"

Sunday, June 30, 2013

365QOD- Day877

"We should never do one on one **training"-Mike**

The other day we had 40 team members in a meeting. During the meeting we discussed many topics and training came up. My ears perked up.

The topic is of interest to me. I love one on one training but I also realize that it creates an interesting problem. I explained it to them.

Suppose I want to train someone to the best of my ability. The trainee will only know at most 80% of what I know about the topic.

Suppose the same employee decides to train a new team member. That person gets 80% of what my trainee learned. By second generation of one on one training that person only knows 64% (.8 *.8=.64) of what I know.

Unless my trainee goes out of their way to get from 80 to 100% then they will pass on the gap to their trainee. So we have to be aware enough to realize after training we must do some self-training. In my opinion, a good rule is that you should spend equal amount to what it takes to do the original training to self-train yourself.

When the group gets the training together then the combined effect is only 80 of what the trainer is capable of and the self-training takes less time.

Today's question is:
"What training gaps have you not filled?"

Tuesday, July 9, 2013

365QOD- Day886

"If you think training people and having them leave is bad, try not training them and having them stay"-unknown

I have worked for companies that believed in training and others that did not. I believe that most companies fall into the second group.

I believe that most companies these days want employees that will show up on day one and be ready to run without ever being instructed on how to walk in their system. This only sets the person up for failure. The company might get some work out of the employee but is it quality work?

In my world, I believe that at least five percent of an employee's time should be spent training. Initially it should start at 100 percent for week one and by the end of the year it should go down to that 5 percent. The training has to be structured and planned not just dependent on the people in similar roles.

So why companies do not chose to do that currently? As the quote instructs, they believe that the person will not work there long enough to make it worth their while. This is why you have to fight for the training you need to be effective in your job.

Today's question is:
"How much do you value on the job training?"

Monday, August 12, 2013

365QOD- Day919

What Are You Reading?

"Read irresponsibly?"- T-shirt slogan

I often ask people around me what they are reading. Sometimes a flood of book names comes out. Most often the person says nothing. That answer always makes me ask them, **"what is the difference between someone who does not read and someone who can't read?"** The sad answer is nothing.

I am constantly reading at least one book at a time. My library allows me to borrow five magazine so I borrow five magazines. My phone has at least one eBook loaded.

The quote above stopped me cold. How does one read irresponsibly? I believe that I do. I read from varied sources and that allows me to see ideas percolate from different fields.

Great ideas have application in more than one area. You just have to look for it. I believe that we have to have new information coming in from different sources in order to be able to generate great ideas.

Today's question is:
"Do you read irresponsibly?"

Saturday, August 17, 2013

365QOD- Day924

It Depends

"There are no stupid questions, only stupid people"-Ernest Chan

Many years ago I was assigned to teach a follow-up class after another professor had crashed and burned. The students hated him and I think he hated them equally.

So I walk in and the first question was, "do you believe there are stupid questions?" I paused for a minute and taught about it. My answer was, "it depends."

I explained to the students that often when learning a new subject we tend to not know enough, and our question might seem stupid to someone who had done it for a while. But and this is the big but, the person has to be willing to allow the questioner to pass through this period.

Now if the person had been doing it for a while and still asks beginner level questions then maybe Ernest's quote is valid. But I still give the person the benefit of a doubt. It might indicate that they were not trained properly. Or even that they have not taken the time to understand what they learned.

Today's question is:
"Do you always ask brilliant questions?"

Monday, August 26, 2013

365QOD- Day933

I will be damned...There is an app for that

"Currently there are over 1 million apps in the Google play store" - a fact as of end of July 2013

Recently I have been studying for PMP certification. I am learning how much more I need to learn when it comes to the subject of Project Management.

Studying for the test has been a blend of trying to memorize a ton of information while thinking about how my company applies the knowledge. Sometimes theory and practice do not even look like they have any similarities.

It is an exciting time for me. But it has also been very difficult. I do not memorize too well. So after reading and reading and cramming I was getting burned out. I decided to look for an app to help me. I was shocked by how many different apps existed to help me with PMP prep.

It made me wonder why I did not look for one or few before starting this process. It would have helped me learn faster and made the memorization a game.

Today's question is:
"Do you look for an app first?"

Sunday, September 1, 2013

365QOD- Day939

Knowledge is NOT Power

"Certainty, knowledge is the lock and the key is the question."- Saf El Sadiq

The expression that knowledge is power is very dangerous. It is not the learning of new that gives us power. The power comes from the application of that knowledge.

Interesting thing about the quote is that in order to get the knowledge we must continue to ask questions. But an interesting thing happens on the way to the question. We don't ask it.

The sad reality is that when we just start learning we are afraid to ask questions so that we do not look foolish. For unknown reason, not looking foolish is more important to us than gaining the knowledge.

On the other extreme is when we are informed and gained some knowledge and we start to believe that we know it all. At this point we do not dare ask a question because we do not want to admit that we still got more to learn.

So the sweet spot is between these two stages. It is the plateau where we tend to not see the improvements we are making and feel the need to continue learning.

Today's question is:
"How do you prolong your questioning plateau?"

Friday, September 6, 2013

365QOD- Day944

Back to the Classroom

"The move to the classroom setting has been critical for MOOC (massive online open courses) for two reasons. For one thing, there is very little money to be made giving a college education away for free. By finding ways to generate revenue from universities, companies like Coursera, might be able to supplement the courses they give away for free. Second of all, universities that have implemented the flipped classroom are seeing impressive results"-Inc. magazine story The future of online education is on campus

The internet has completely changed the way we work and learn. Can you imagine a workday during which you do not use the internet? I would argue that probably most of internet use is for personal reasons and if work gets done then that is a side benefit.

Now education is also changing. I wrote about how I thought that in the near future the students would listen to prerecorded lectures from authors/experts and work on quizzes at home. This would enable homework to be done in the classroom. In addition, application of the material can be done with the teacher.

I also previously wrote how I was surprised to learn that enormous number of students that sign up for MOOC drop out. Even though the courses are free, the effort to stay with the course is great. They might be interested in the material but not very committed to finish.

So a blended education of free online content with a mix of flipped content might be the answer. It looks like universities are willing to play along and pay for expert lectures while providing a setting for learning to take place.

Today's question is:
"Would a flipped classroom model with free online education work for you?"

Monday, September 30, 2013

365QOD- Day968

One Article per Magazine

"Too much data. I am overwhelmed."-my conclusion

This morning I ran an experiment. I have several magazines as shortcut on my desktop. I went to each one and selected a single article of interest. Then I copied the article into a word document.

Selecting a single article from seven magazines added up to twenty pages of content. Wow! I did not think it would be that much. Now the bigger question is, are the articles worth the time needed to read them?

The articles were very specific to me. Most likely it will take an hour to read and process the data into information. For me these will be sources for blog posts so it is the diet needed to keep the blog going.

I suspect that most people tend to read anywhere from 20 to 100 pages of content from the Web each day. If the effort is focused then it is of value. But if the reading is on a starlet breakdown then it is simply wasted time.

Today's question us:
"How much content do you read each day?"

Saturday, October 5, 2013

365QOD- Day973

Too Many Questions

"Life is too short to be wasted in finding answers. Enjoy the questions!"-Paulo Coelho

One of these days I am going to take all of the questions from my blog and put them in one document and reread them out loud. I believe it will be hard to just read them.

By now you should know that I enjoy posing questions to think about. Rarely do I get upset if the answer does not pop out immediately. I do not expect it. If it is a worthwhile question then the answer will also take time to arrive.

So how does one enjoy the question? I believe that by letting go and not expecting the answer is the way to enjoy the question. I also think that this also places the question in our subconscious. So your brain is really working on the question when you do not think you are working on it.

Unfortunately we are often too eager to ask our next question that we might not even hear the answer. It is the pause that allows the answer to come up.

Today's question is:
"Can you enjoy the delay to the answer?"

Monday, October 28, 2013

365QOD- Day996

Learning or Winning

"The great ones treat failure as a necessary part of their journey. It's not win or lose. It's always win or learn," says Eric Lefkofsky, CEO of Groupon

I love the line it is always win or learn. If you look at experiences as just that then what do we have to worry about. Either we will win or we will learn.

The win might have taken several learning steps to reach. It is not guaranteed to occur on our first attempt. But we should be able to bring it closer in our future attempts by examining each attempt and making intelligent adjustments. That is the premise of my first book, The Result.

We should always learn from our non-wins as we should not take too much credit for our wins. Be humble and keep working and learning should always be out motto.

Today's question is:
"Do you always learn if you don't win?"

Tuesday, November 19, 2013

365QOD- Day1018

One and Done

"I do not want to do this again."- My thought during my PMP exam

Yesterday I took my PMP exam. PMP exam consists of 200 questions that you must answer in four hours. It was probably the second hardest test I have taken in my life. The hardest being the qualifying exams for Ph.D.

The knowledge behind the test is something that I do every day. I manage people and projects. So getting a Project Management Professional certification is not too far of a stretch. It makes sense to understand the framework of how to manage large projects and certify that you understand it.

What makes the PMP test so hard then? Well, it is a multiple choice test so you are guaranteed the monkey score of 25% even if you do not know anything. The problem with the test is that most of the choices were in the "gray area". To answer the questions not only did you have to understand what they wanted but most likely have applied it. Book smart folks could pass the test but it is very unlikely in my opinion that without experience you can pass it.

The benefit of taking the test was the preparation for it. It immersed me into the framework for doing projects and I started noticing the knowledge creeping into my every day conversations. It is good to stretch ones knowledge and then test yourself to see if you mastered it.

I did pass the exam.

Today's question is:

"What is a learning challenge you are trying to overcome?"

Learning from others

Saturday, August 24, 2013

365QOD- Day931

No Pain...No Lesson

"A lot of **epiphanies come at the end of an unpleasant process. That process is not only necessary to achieve the epiphany, but part of the epiphany itself. As such, distilling that process down to an axiom isn't as valuable as going through the process itself, however grueling it might** be."- Unknown

This is the answer to the question, **"What is a life changing realization that you wish you'd had sooner?"** on the suite Ask Metafilter. I believe the advice offers a lot of wisdom.

We want the learning process to be easy. Well, as I have said before, if it is easy then it is worth nothing. If I tell you a fact for which I paid dearly it does not mean the same to you. It cannot.

If you are lucky then you will remember it in the short term as good advice but in the long run you will forget it. Why? Because as the quote teaches you did not go through the process where you discovered it. The process is a part of the discovery, the epiphany. Without the process, your temporary gain is only temporary.

This is kind of sad when you think about it. It means that others can teach us but we must still go through the process to ingrain the fact. The best we will be able to do is to speed up our learning but not eliminate it.

Maybe this is why kids repeat the mistakes of their parents even though the parent tries to prevent the pain?

Today's question us:
"Have you had an epiphany without going through the process?"

Monday, February 18, 2013

365QOD- Day744

"You should focus on being interested rather than interesting"- Jacqueline Novogratz

I believe there is a reason why our human body is designed with two ears and one mouth. In my opinion, this design allows us to be able to listen to others twice as much as we talk.

Unfortunately, the reality is that we tend to talk twice as much as we listen. Often times we only just hear enough before wanting to jump in and comment.

So what?

Well, by listening we are working on the first part of the quote- 'being interested'. We give the other person an opportunity to give us a view of their world and beliefs.

By actively listening and being interested, provides us some room to sound off and be interesting to the other person. If you truly hear what they are saying then you are better going to be able to reach them.

Today's question is:
"How do you show you are being interested?"

Sunday, February 24, 2013

365QOD- Day750

"What is it with people?" - My question

Something that I have observed in the last year drives me nuts. People are just completely unaware of the physical space around them. I do not know if it is a cell phone phenomenon or not BUT I see the same when people are not attached to their phones.

People just seem to just stop without consideration for anyone around them. They just stop as if they are lost. They care less if they are in anyone's way. The bump into things and people without apologizing.

I do not know if they are in deep thought or not BUT it seems like someone has turned off a switch or two. It is making me wonder if I am doing the same thing. Everything is more annoying when someone else does it.

Today's question is:
"Are some of your switches turned OFF?"

Thursday, July 4, 2013

365QOD- Day881

"If you ask the wrong question, the answer does not matter. Dare to risk-
because in the new world, risky is the new safe."- Randy Gage author of Risky is the New Safe

This blog is based on the premise of generating great questions to ask oneself. I usually formulate the question after the post has been written so that it is relevant. Hopefully, I am not asking the wrong question?

The idea of asking the wrong question is very interesting to me. I believe that it is possible to reach a wrong conclusion and based on that ask the wrong question. Maybe it is more than that?

I believe that, as the book title indicates, another way you can ask the wrong question is by playing it safe. By asking the wrong question you might not want to rock the boat. You do not want the other affected people to feel threatened by your question. So you settle for the easy question.

Today's question is:
"How do you know that you did not ask the wrong question?"

Monday, December 2, 2013
365QOD- Day1031

Moments

"MoHI- moments of high impact"- Paul Balmert

I spent today in safety leadership training by Paul. It was excellent. I am definitively looking forward to the second day.

During the class Paul did a demonstration of how we see incidents and at times we miss critical moments that have great influence. He calls these MoHIs. These are moments, if used properly, can improve the leadership position of a leader with respect to his followers.

What was interesting to me was how often we tend to miss these moments. He even quantifies them as low, medium, and high. In the example he shared it was difficult to label them properly. The lesson for me is to use any moment and improve its MoHI potential by noting who the followers are and how to move them.

The key is to stay open and recognize moments as they are occurring. I believe that this becomes easier with practice.

Today's question is:
"Can you recognize MoHI moments?"

Life Mission

Sunday, June 16, 2013

365QOD- Day863

"1000 days out of 21000 "- My countdown

6/7/13 is the 1000th day since I awoke. My countdown started on 9/12/10 in a bar while on a solo vacation in Florida. I decided that I wanted to live 21000 days- till age 101.

Recently, I spent a day reflecting on the changes since that day. As a matter of fact most are probably chronicled in previous posts.

In the last 1000 days I have:
Ran in several 5k, 10k, 20k(13.1mi) races
Changed jobs
Got promoted
Moved from Indiana to Texas
Continued writing my blog
Published a second book
(Finishing my third book)
Taught myself how to create apps
Published an app
Vacationed for a month overseas
Etc.

They have been busy 1000 days. Maybe I could and should have done more?

I spent some time thinking about my next checkup. Should I review my life every 1000, 500,250,200, or 100 days? Should it be at the end of a month or end of year only?

I concluded that yearly is too long. 500 or 1000 are also too long. Similarly, I also believe that for me it needs to be in terms of days and not months.

So, I have decided that every 200 days (a bit longer than six months) to stop for a day and do a review of my life. During the review not only review the successes but also the failures. I will also review if I am on the path to achieving the big goals in my life. The day will be spent reflecting.

Today's question is:
"How often do you reflect on your life?"

Tuesday, June 18, 2013

365QOD- Day865

"Is it?" -my question to myself

On my wall is a sign that states, "The Year of The App". Besides publishing an app a few months ago I have not been working on any new ones lately.

Because I often like to tackle many things I periodically have to ask myself,
    "**Is it still important?**"
Or even better,
    "**Why am I creating this product?**"

Amazingly enough when I read article on 99u.com the founder of Jawbone Hosain Rahman he asks himself these same two questions. It is his way of cutting though the noise and a way to revisit his core principles.

My answer about the apps is yes and that once I am done with my next two projects I will spend the last three months creating new apps. I do need to change my sign to The Year of Some Apps.

Today's question is:
"**How do you decide what is still important?**"

Friday, July 12, 2013
365QOD- Day889

"It is my birthday..it is my birthday"- My first words today

Today is my birthday. I turned 47. Another 54 years to go. Not even half way.

Did I do anything special? I went to work and went out to dinner. Not bad...

What made the day memorable was the yearly pause I do. I pause to think about if the gap between where I am and where I want to be is getting smaller or larger. The answer this year is that it is smaller. What this means that the direction is correct but the speed might need to be increased. In physics the combined term that is used for these two concepts is velocity.

Today's question is:
"Are your direction AND speed correct?"

Thursday, July 18, 2013

365QOD- Day894

"Where is it that you do not want to be in five years?"- A great question

A few weeks ago I read an article on interviewing in Inc. magazine. This is one of the suggested questions to ask a prospective hire. Why? Most people do not have a canned answer for it.

I also feel it is a great question but maybe for a different reason. I believe it is a great question to ask ourselves at least once a month. Where do you want to be in five years and equally important where you do not want to be?

I believe that most people will answer quickly by saying not here. But that is not really a good answer. It is not specific enough for you to tell where you actually want to be. Usually the opposite of what you do not want is what you really want.

You have to clearly identify it as something definite that you do not want. Remember that God has a sense of humor, so if you are not clear you will get something that has elements of what you want with elements of what you do not want.

Today's question is:
"Where is it that you do not want to be in five years?"

Wednesday, September 25, 2013

365QOD- Day963

Vacation Goals

"Vacation without a creative goal is a wasted vacation."-according to me

I have spent the last few weeks on vacation. It was not as good as my vacation last year but it gave me some time to stop and pause. This is something we have to do in order to appreciate the music notes of our lives.

But going on vacation does not mean just sitting there vegetating. Ok, I confess that I did veg out a bit. But I was also productive creatively.

Last summer I taught myself how to write an Android app. Later on in the year I developed an app and made it available for free at the Google Play store.

This year's focus was to develop different products. So mentioned in another recent post I wrote 52 small eBooks. I also read a little about marketing and LinkedIn. I believe that marketing of self and products thru LinkedIn will develop into a monster on the order of Amazon.

It was also a time to think about some life goals and strategies. Our lives tend to be too busy to have a lot of free time to think about those. So this time allowed me to sip a bit of coffee and to reflect.

Today's question is:
"Do you set vacation goals?"

Thursday, January 30, 2014

365QOD- Day1089

5 Million Dollar Loan

"What would I do with it?"- My question to myself

Last night a friend of mine mentioned to me a process by which one can obtain a 5 million loan. The repayment of the loan does not start for 18 months. My ears perked up.

I have never in my life envisioned having a brick and mortar business. My ideal business would not involve directly manufacturing anything. Most likely it would involve a small team that does not have to be in a single office in order to produce products that can be supported by me.

So what his story did was made me question myself. If money availability was taken off the table, what would I do? Would I think differently and do a brick and mortar type of business? Or would I stick with my current plans?

To me money has never been a limiting factor. I have never felt that I needed more resources then what I have to fund the execution of an idea. But I know for many people this is a big stumbling block. With sites like KickStarter and others if you have a great idea then you will get the money to execute it.

I believe that the most precious resource for me is time. I can never get enough of it. So the answer for me is that I would do the same things I am doing now as side projects but only do them full time. The money would simply replace my income.

What about you?

Today's question is:

"What business idea would you pursue if you were given a 5 million dollar loan?"

Making Mistakes

Thursday, February 21, 2013

365QOD- Day747

"All Advice is autobiographical It is one of my theories that when people give advice, they are really just talking to themselves in the past. This book is me talking to a previous version of myself."- Austin Kleon Steel Like an Artist book

We are so full of opinions. When presented with a story we jump at the chance to offer advice. Hell, sometimes we don't even wait to hear the whole story.

This desire to solve the other person's problem stems from the quote. We are in a sense giving our younger selves advice. It is as if we are solving our own past problems with new information gathered from experience. We cannot wait to fix a younger version of ourselves.

Today's question is:
"What is the best advice would you give your younger self?"

Thursday, February 28, 2013

365QOD-Day754

"Bad choices make good stories" - t-shirt slogan

I believe in learning to make better mistakes. It is silly to make the same mistake over and over again. It seems that you are just not awake if you make the same mistake repeatedly. You are not living in the present.

When I saw this t-shirt I immediately wrote it down. I sometimes try to remember slogans and later realize that it is a mistake because I cannot recover them. So I took my phone out and wrote it in a file called quotes. I did not make the same mistake again. I made a better choice.

Another part of this slogan is the storytelling aspect. I believe that most of us want to hide our mistakes. BUT if we could allow ourselves to share the mistakes we will definitely tell a good story that others will easily remember and maybe not make the same mistake. It also makes us more human to others.

Today's question is:
"Do you tell good stories?"

Mastery

Tuesday, June 11, 2013

365QOD- Day858

"I stand on the shoulders of giants"- giving credit

My first book, **The Result,** is a true story. The idea behind the book is that you always get a result and not to call it failure or success comes from Tony Robbins. So my book is an application of the idea.

This morning I was reading an article on 99u.com site that discusses the idea of plateaus on the path to mastery. The author does a good job of describing the types of personalities and their behavior when confronted by a plateau.

Unfortunately the author does not give credit for the idea originator. If you get a hold of the book Mastery by George Leonard you will discover the identical types. The only difference is that George applied them generally while the author applied it to tennis.

The reason I bring this up is not to put down the author. It is for us to realize and credit a source. Maybe I did not acknowledge the giant as well as I should for my book? I have to go back and re-read a part of my book.

Today's question is:
" Whose shoulder does your idea stand on?"

Wednesday, July 10, 2013

365QOD- Day 887

"What is the opposite of the mastery curve called?"-my question to a coworker

Carrie walked in and told me a story about a movie called Perfect Senses. In the movie people deal with the loss of one sense one at a time.

While she was telling me the story I kept visualizing the challenges. Immediately I saw each loss as a step down. With each step, the person goes through a brief rough patch, even dips below the step, and eventually rests on the plateau.

This is the reverse of what George Leonard wrote about in his book Mastery. As the person rises in levels they experience a rise above the plateau level with eventually resting on the plateau. On the path to mastery the plateaus get longer and longer with smaller step changes between levels.

For the opposite idea, I can imagine with each loss, the plateau would also get longer. Maybe the loss of taste is not as critical as loss of hearing. Maybe the loss of hearing is not as bad as loss of vision, etc.

So what is the opposite of mastery stair steps? The word I came up with is coping steps. You are adjusting to losses.

Today's question is:
"Are you coping or mastering?"

Sunday, November 17, 2013

365QOD- Day1016

Eliminating or Adding Steps

"Toyota is known for eliminating any steps that are intermediary or unimportant"- Tim Ferriss

Many times we tend to make things for complex by adding steps. Companies are very good at adding hurdles on the path to execution. They do not tolerate risk and by including extra steps they feel that they have better control of the system. However, this often creates frustration because it lacks common sense of what needs to be done in order to execute a job.

The quote illustrates that some of the most efficient companies do the opposite. They want to eliminate the unnecessary work and steps in order to get better quality. To most American companies the extra steps are needed to guarantee quality.

I believe that intermediate steps are needed in order to assure people know why a particular step is needed. This is very obvious when one watches a martial artist perform a kata form. Most forms consist of anywhere from 10+ to 100 individual steps. Just remembering the steps for some of the complex ones requires months and years of learning. The level of knowing how to do one without thought takes even more time.

Eventually, you learn the pattern and you can perform it without mistakes. This is just information that has become knowledge. It is not mastery.

So what does it take to transition from knowledge to wisdom?

Mastery requires one to go back and look at the intermediate steps that are missing. As an example consider that the transition from one position to another requires the turning of the head from current position to the new position without turning the body. This is awkward for most students. However, would you ever turn the body into danger before you have to by simply rotating the head to see what is coming at you from that direction? Most students do so because they do not know the intermediate steps.

Today's question is:

"Do you know the purpose of the intermediate steps of your job?"

Memorable

Wednesday, February 27, 2013

365QOD-Day753

"I am changed again"- My response to a book

A couple of years ago I read a book called Ka-Ching. It opened my eyes to the world of creating a blog and publishing. The end result was two books and a daily blog which keeps turning out new material. The book was so powerful that I could not even wait to finish it without starting the blog. I had to do it while finishing the book.

This weekend I read the book iPhone Millionaire. It blew me away. I had just got done with another book which I thought was one of the best books I have ever read so I did not expect this one to move me. But move me it did.

In the iPhone Millionaire the author, Michael Rosenblum, clearly lays out the case for videos being more and more in demand and the key to the next opportunity wave. The book teaches you how to become a better photographer, videographer, and creator of videos. It even touches on how to sell yourself and your work.

It made me wonder how to incorporate it in my success formula. My current multiple streams of income are: blog, books, apps, and now videos. The combination and mission need to support my ultimate need to create. I do not have the answers now BUT I know that my world will never be the same. I have not been able to stop talking about the book since I finished reading it. (Maybe I should have started shooting videos already?)

Today's question is:
"Have you ever been changed by a book?"

Thursday, March 7, 2013

365QOD-Day761

"Wow.. here it is"- My surprise

On Saturday I walked into a Whole Foods grocery store. This is my second time to walk into this brand store.

What I noticed surprised me. As I walked down the aisle I saw price tags that were adaptive. The price could be changed electronically instead of replacing a paper tag with another paper tag. The electronic change could be done adaptively from an office by an algorithm.

You are probably wondering, "So what!" Well, this was an idea that I considered implementing almost 10 years ago. I could see the writing on the wall that all stores would need to go to this system. I do not know why I lost interest in the idea. The idea was brilliant but my execution was non-existent.

How many of my ideas do I see like this? Unfortunately many...

Recently I was in a Forever21 department store. They have a million articles that are marked down. Women are fighting through a million dresses without any order. The items are not sorted at all but thrown in different rooms. It has to be a nightmare for the store when they want to change the price of an item.

The adaptive price tag is the answer to all of their troubles. I wonder if they know it even exists.

Today's question is:
"How do you force yourself to execute a brilliant idea?"

Friday, March 15, 2013

365QOD- Day769

"Copyright infringement for free eBooks?" - An idea

I recently read an article in MIT press. It described a company that someone started to make free ebooks that mimic the topics and presentation in most popular books. It has gotten sued by major publishers.

So the idea is you take the table of contents from a popular book and the company does a search on Wikipedia to extract the topics and create a book that mimics the flow and information.

It made me wonder if a flow of a book is patentable. For example, if I am teaching a course I would follow the table of contents pretty closely because the order makes intuitive sense. Yes you can vary the flow a little by moving topics but for overall coverage in most classes the flow will not change that much.

Today's question is:
"Could you create a book, on a subject of interest, for yourself based on a Wikipedia or web contents?"

Wednesday, April 10, 2013
365QOD - Day795

"Now I got something to test it with"- My words

Recently I started reading a book called **Laptop Millionaire**. While I was reading it I had an idea. Instead of just reading the book and saying what a great book full of ideas it is, I decided to stop reading it until I can just apply it.

Well most of the products that I am working on did not fit so I decided to create a new product. What!

I wrote a workbook in two days that is about 175 pages long. Yup! In two days. If you want something bad enough then just do it instead of looking for excuses. Now I can simply test the concept instead of just reading and wondering if the ideas actually work.

Today's question is:
"What price are you willing to pay to test an idea?"

Thursday, May 23, 2013

365QOD- Day839

"Pay attention to the little things people do." - My words to myself

Many years ago I learned a valuable lesson. I shared an office with a co-worker. He was younger than me and I helped train him. He did not directly work for me. We shared an office and a desktop computer. I also had a laptop that was issued to me.

Over time I noticed that he would take things that did not belong to him as if it was issued to him. If I left a dollar on my desk, it became his. Any tool that I had became his. Since the desktop was company property I could not complain. However, on the desktop I had some personal files for my part time teaching job.

One week I left to teach a plant course on SPC and when I came back he had moved out of the office and taken the desktop. I went to his new office and asked to retrieve my personnel files. He said that he completely wiped the computer clean and destroyed my files.

I was pissed. I did not care if he moved out or if he took the desktop but the files he destroyed took a lot of effort to create. When I confronted his boss he just shrugged his shoulders.

The lesson I learned that day was to look at the little things that people do and extrapolate **(predict)** potential future problems with that individual. I should have noted his and his boss' behavior and lack of boundaries when it came to assigned equipment and predicted that he could do something like what he ended up doing.

Today's question is:
" Do you extrapolate future actions from the small things people do?"

Thursday, June 27, 2013

365QOD- Day874

"If you want to achieve excellence, you can get there today. As of this second, quit doing less than excellent work " - Thomas J. Watson

Long time ago I listened to a book by Jim Rohn in which he makes a statement that change only takes a second but that moment often takes a lifetime to get to. This statement by Watson immediately reminded me of it.

Even though one of the quotes talks about change and the other about quality they are both talking about a decision. A decision to choose. To choose a better way over an easy path.

What drives that decision? I believe that events can force us or we can evolve beyond our current state. My definition of a state is the level you have reached in physical, mental, emotional, spiritual, financial, etc. dimensions.

In my world we are always better off choosing and thus evolving rather to be forced by circumstances.

Today's question is:
"How do you evolve beyond your current state?"

Sunday, August 11, 2013

365QOD- Day918

Ding...

"When it rings, ask yourself if you spent your last hour productively."-
the 18minute ritual that will boost your productivity article in Entrepreneur magazine

For the last two weeks I have been running an experiment with myself. I have downloaded an app called Mindfulness Bell and set it to ring every hour randomly. The interval can be adjusted to more often or less often.

So during the last two weeks every time the mindfulness bell went off I would focus myself on my breathing for one minute. At the end of the minute, I measured my pulse by using my watch. The goal is to get my pulse to be in the low sixties. Ultimately my goal is to have my pulse in the low sixties for one whole day.

Since the bell is set to randomly go off, it has gone off at some interesting times such as meetings. I do not acknowledge the bell and quietly start my breathing. Most people around me assume that it is an email alert or simply an alarm. They do not notice the change in my breathing pattern.

My latest addition to this procedure is the idea from the quote above. After the pulse check I ask myself if the last hour was productive. Did I wisely use the 3600 "presents" that I was given in the last hour? Sometimes the answer is no and that is enough to raise my pulse. I then realize that next hour is an opportunity to be more mindful.

Today's question is:
"Do you pause ever hour to breathe and reflect?"

Thursday, September 5, 2013

365QOD- Day943

Go Go Speed Racer...go NeuroRacer

" In a groundbreaking new study at the University of California, San Francisco, scientists found that older adults improved cognitive controls such as multitasking and the ability to sustain attention by playing a specially designed video game — and that the effects can be long lasting.

The study, to be published in the scientific journal Nature on Thursday, is part of a broader effort to understand whether specially designed video games can help treat neurological disorders, such as attention-deficit hyperactivity disorder and even depression.

There is growing evidence, researchers say that videogames could eventually become therapies on par, or used in tandem, with ingestible medications."- Wall Street Journal

I read this story and immediately smiled. Something, video games, that had often been thought of as wasteful and harmful to the brain is now beneficial. If used strategically this could be a game changer.

In the story elderly folks who played the game did better than twenty year olds for six months after the training. This was after the training stopped.

So if we could play a game specially designed for us we could attack mental issues. Imagine a game that could attack attention deficit disorders or Alzheimer. Or the simple middle age short term memory failure.

The potential is endless.

Today's question is:
"What would a game designed for you help you with?"

Tuesday, September 17, 2013

365QOD- Day955

A Great Day

"Would you know a great day if you saw one?"- Advice given to Jason Womack by his mentor

I recently was reading some stories from different sources when this little gem popped out. I immediately knew that I had to write a post about it.

When I first started numbering my days I quickly realized that most days are not memorable. We have to make strategic choices in order to make them memorable. If we are not aware enough then the day slips into the past without a trace.

I also realized that for me a day without creativity can never be a great day. It can be a fulfilling and productive day. But only days when I produce something creative are great days.

This is why the quote resonated with me. I have a very tight specific criteria to make a day into a great day. I suspect that most people would not be able to create a great day. Maybe even a large number would not even recognize one if they saw one.

Today's question is:
"What is your great day criteria?"

Sunday, October 6, 2013

365QOD- Day974

Both Sides are Idiots

"I hate both political parties equally."-my words

I am saddened that the two parties are full of politicians that are holding our country hostage. This is not what our founding fathers intended. Consider a few issues.

The country needs a basic health plan. I do not think it should take 2000 pages that no one has read to formulate it. There is no western country without basic health care plan. Why are we different? Because medical lobbyists write the laws and politicians get paid by them.

Our medical system is broken. When someone without insurance goes to an emergency room for basic care then all of our costs go up. Do young people need the same coverage as elderly or middle age folks? No. So a plan needs to be formulated for 20-30 year old and older people that is different and cheap.

The other issue is spending. It is amazing to me that when either party is in power that they do not decide to control spending. For example, the Republicans like their wars and police actions around the world. We have gone from the most admitted nation to the most hated in the last 30 years.

The Democrats like their social programs. This is their way of employing more people that will vote for them next election. By spending on programs that do not work, they prevent the creation of programs that will work.

Neither party cares about the little working guy. They give lip service. What they care about it getting reelected. If they do not follow their own party line they will get kicked out by their own. They serve the party not us. Thus is why an Obama white house member said that "they are winning" on this government shutdown. They care about getting reelected more than fixing the problems. Sad.

Our forefathers wanted statesmen who would argue the issues and do what is best for the country. They were intending for people to go to Washington for a few years and dedicate themselves for the best of the country.

This is not what we got now. We have a group of people that only care to last long enough to get their pension and lifelong medical. This is because they see it as a job instead of service to the country. We deserve better.

Today's question is:
"Would you be willing to vote out every currently elected official?"

Saturday, October 19, 2013

365QOD- Day987

"Me and my shadow"-words to a song

I was reading an online version of Inc. magazine and came across a story about Jeff Bezos. In the story it tells how Jeff has a person who is assigned to shadow him and serve as his sounding board.

Some of his shadows held that position for a few years and then became a CEO of a division. This is a brilliant way to develop the shadow in the way you feel will set them up for success.

In the story Jeff tells that shadow success is defined by each person getting to know the other and then developing trust. This is very risky since the shadow can then find an executive position elsewhere.

I love this idea but unless you are the CEO how do you apply this idea? I believe that a younger coworker might be interested in becoming a shadow of a more senior employee. The senior takes the shadow to meetings and then asks them for feedback. What went good and what went bad?

If both agree to get to know each other and trust each other's opinion then both will grow. It does not have to be full time either. I say 20% of time overlap is ideal.

Today's question is:
"Would a shadow be beneficial to your development?"

Sunday, October 20, 2013

365QOD- Day988

Overchallenging

"Do I need to go down and get my certificate that says I am the CEO of this company to get you to stop challenging me in this?"-Jeff Bezos being a jerk

While reading a story in an online issue of Entrepreneur I came across a story that talked about how Bezos like Jobs is a jerk sometimes to his employees. So why did this catch my attention?

I happen to have a boss with whom I differ on strategy very often. We even disagree publicly. I don't disagree without being respectful. He is the boss.

I might disagree and challenge my boss but the winner is our company. If ideas are challenged and the best ones implemented then the winner is our company. As long as the company wins then there is no such thing as too much challenging. If a boss has to pull out his certificate then that speaks of their weakness in persuading others that their idea is the best.

Today's question is:
"Do you over challenge?"

Monday, October 21, 2013

365QOD- Day989

The Triangle

"Leaders need to know when to become followers and followers need to know when to become leaders."- Jim Collins, business guru

While reading the latest issue of Inc. I noticed an article about Jim Collins and his teaching at West Point. While at West Point he noticed that leadership model that they follow can be thought of as a triangle. One point of the triangle is made up of **Success**; second point is **Growth**, and the last one **Service**.

A leader has to want Success. You have to believe that it is achievable. And you have to want to do your personal best to reach success. This is all just a belief.

While you are reaching for Success you will taste failure. Failure is inevitable. But learning from it is optional. However, it is learning from it that will lead to Growth. This is feedback.

The last piece is Service. Without wanting to pull people along on the journey towards success, the journey is not as fulfilling. Wanting success for them is just as important as wanting success for yourself. This is caring for others.

Today's question is:
"Do you believe in the triangle leadership model?"

Tuesday, October 22, 2013

365QOD- Day990

Meaningful Life

"It is very difficult to have a great life unless it is a meaningful life. And it is very difficult to have a meaningful life without meaningful work, or to have meaningful work without all the legs of the triangle."-Jim Collins

In post I described the legs of the triangle: Success, Growth, and Service. This quote comes from the same article on Jim's teaching at West Pointe and leadership.

The easy way to visualize this quote is:
```
Success   => Meaningful=>Meaningful => Great
Growth       Work        Life          Life
Service
```

Maybe I am wrong but I do not self-identify with the work that I currently do. It is meaningful work BUT it is not my life. Don't get me wrong, I care about being successful, growing, and being of service to others. I even enjoy it but it is not leading me to a meaningful life.

There have been times when I felt that my work at that time, teaching at a major university, was leading me to a meaningful life. And maybe if I had stayed on that path it would have led to a great life. Maybe? The difficulty was making a living at which you can thrive instead of just survive.

Currently, writing and creating gives me the meaningful work and meaningful life. I believe that it will eventually lead to a great life. A life where I spend most of my time creatively.

Today's question is:
"Do you believe that your current work could lead to a great life?"

Wednesday, October 23, 2013

365QOD- Day991

Designing a Life

"Life is meant to be designed- most people just react or fly by the seat of their pants."-Lauren Zander

I believe in destiny. There have been too many instances in my life where I have seen evidence of the fingerprints of God. With this said, I do believe that Lauren is correct.

We are given a free will to do with our lives what we wish. There will even be instances when we make choices that are self-destructive. I believe that most of us fit the second part of that quote in that we either react or fly by the sit of our pants.

Even with the help of God's fingerprints, we are responsible to design the life that we want. Many years ago I sat for an hour brainstormed a perfect life. I can tell you that at times portions of that vision were realized but never completely.

A couple of years ago I redid this exercise and what came out was completely different vision of what my life should look like. The life I would design today is different than the life I would have designed in my late twenties or thirties.

Life design could result in a separate blog or book by itself. In this one post, I want you to think about whether you are the designer of your life or just a spectator.

Today's question is:
"Are you a spectator or an active designer of your life?"

Friday, November 1, 2013

365QOD- Day1000

Today marks an important milestone. To me to do something for 1000 days continuously is impressive. I believe that it has taught me to think and do differently.
I just want to say THANKS for visiting and following the blog. Hopefully your journey leads you to your desired destination.

Millionaire at 15

"Is it what she thinks or how she thinks?"-Tommy Hendricks

The inspiration for today's post came from episode of Shark Tank. A mom and two girls walk in and the oldest of the two tells about the business she came up with when she was 10 to sell trinkets made from bottle caps. Her contribution to the "economy of stupid" lead to her earning 1.6 million in sales of which profit was 1 million.

I told Tommy this story and we both were impressed and wondered about her thinking process. Immediately, Tommy wondered what made her think the way she does or even better how she thinks.

My thoughts were more on the execution side. What made her execute her ideas and led to her success? I am sure many young kids have ideas but their ideas are usually in their head and if they are lucky they make it to paper. But usually that is as far as they go.

To execute something, like she her sister and mom have, great requires the willingness to pay the price. You have to be willing to go from thinking to doing and move to doing it every day even when you don't feel like it.

I believe that that is the lesson of writing a big for a thousand days: become disciplined to do something for an extended amount of time and not quit. I do not believe that I am the same person that stated this journey a thousand days ago.

Thanks for your support...

Today's question is:
"What would you become after doing something for a thousand days?"

Day 1148 out of 21000(Refer to post 12 for the meaning)

Tuesday, November 5, 2013

365QOD- Day1004

Leading From the Side

"Don't lead me, I'll wonder off. Don't follow me, I'll get you lost. Walk beside me and help me cause trouble."- unknown

I found this quote while checking my Facebook page. Immediately I noticed the uniqueness. Is this a way to lead?

You often are taught that we should lead from a front position. We have to have vision and hopefully the team will follow us on the journey. Unfortunately, many leaders that lead from the front do not bother to look behind to see if they are followed. They assume because of their positional leadership that people should just follow them. That is not always the case. As I always say, "If you are leader without followers, then you are just taking a walk."

Leading from behind is another way that people believe that one should lead a team. BUT I have never found this to be effective. It is better to lead from up front than to lead from behind. People believe that they are pulling you along and since you are the leader than they lose faith in you. No one will follow people that hide in the back of the pack.

The wisdom in this quote is the leading from the side. Walk beside me and help me cause trouble. I love it! This fits my style. I lead by allowing myself to stray off the beaten path and getting people to follow their instincts that the journey off the path is truly the best path. I don't have to convince them because they convince themselves.

Do you know what is another word for trouble? Change.

Today's question is:
"Do you ever lead from the side?"

Saturday, November 9, 2013

365QOD- Day1008

Delayed Life Plan

"If I could just have X then I would get Y."-my version

We always think in terms of this equation. For example, have you ever said," if I only had time I would finish my project." Or, "if I had money I would build my project." Substitute whatever word is relevant for you instead of project. This statement creates a life delay.

The biggest delay in our life that we fool ourselves with is that we can work a whole life unhappy in jobs and relationships and at the end we will live out Nirvana. Nirvana for most people is being retired and traveling the world.

Foolish!

In an old post I shared some wisdom given to Jim Rohn. When Jim Rohn said to his mentor that, "if he had money, he would have a plan." His adviser, Earl, reversed it by advising that "if he had a plan he would get the money." The response is full of great wisdom.

Maybe by doing the project you will get excited and squeeze in the time? Maybe if you do the project, the money will show up? Maybe if you travel and enjoy life you will find Nirvana now? The answer is if you do the Y then X will come.

Today's question is:
"What are your Y and X?"

Sunday, November 10, 2013

365QOD- Day1009

Recording Your World

"GoPro"- name for a camera

Many years ago I wondered what it would be like to record my life. Immediately I concluded that a pair of glasses with tiny cameras mounted on the side would serve the purpose. At that point I knew that all it would take is time for those cameras to come onto the market. As I said this was a thought I had many years ago.

In the mean time I read of a Microsoft scientist who caries around a camera around his neck. The camera with many sensors records his life. Wonderful idea. He can reduce a day into fifteen minutes and review. So if you take 365*.25=91.25 hours to review a year. What would you do with that review?

Google glasses is another version of this idea. It however adds the ability see a computer screen in front of you. So not only do you record your life but you can also surf.

Tonight on 60 minutes I watched a segment on the GoPro cameras and what people are doing with them. There is a whole movement to record cool and crazy things that people are doing. Mostly athletic endeavors but also some silly and fun life happenings. It made the inventor one of the newest billionaires in the USA.

I still believe that what I envisioned is a great idea. Someone will eventually produce it. Now is the time.

Today's question is:
"Would you record your world?"

Tuesday, November 26, 2013

365QOD- Day1025

Making a Dent in the Universe

"We're here to put a dent in the universe. Otherwise, why else even be here?"- Steve Jobs

Have you ever wondered why you are here? What is the meaning of your life? When the life candle burns out, what will the people left behind think was your purpose? What dents did you make?

I believe that my mission is to influence others to do better. When I was a teacher for 18 years I influenced several thousand students in seven institutions. I believe that most if not all were better off for having me as a teacher. Most would probably say that I was very different than most of their teachers in getting them to think outside the box.

Today, I influence through my work in industry and my creative writings. Every day I write about a topic that peaks my interest. I hope that it resonates with others. Again, I am trying to think outside their comfort box.

I also believe that having a higher purpose doesn't just help you find success. But finding it, it helps redefine the meaning of the word. My highest value is to creativity. My mission and highest value match up pretty well.

Today's question is:
"How will you make a dent in the Universe?"

Wednesday, December 18, 2013

365QOD- Day1047

Being of Service Costs

"Service is the rent we pay for living."- Marian Wright Edelman, The Measure of Our Success

The other day I was reading an article about books that changed people's lives. One of the people referenced this book and this line. It jumped out of the rest of the article to capture my attention.

What does it mean that we pay rent for living? I do not think God is sitting up there getting ready to collect. At least God does not do this in my world view.

But I like this line as a reminder. We should be of service to others as a way of belonging here. We pay rent in order to realize that we appreciate our life. Why? How many things that were given to you that were free that you marvel at and appreciate? Most often you said Thanks and moved on. But if you paid the price then you will remember it.

So being of service is important. It keeps the agreement that we made with each other that we will help and love one another. At least that is what I do in my world view. I love the way Zig Ziegler used to say this, **"In this world you can have anything in life you want, if you will just help other people get what they want."** That is service to many! Be of service to many and all of your wants will be filled.

Today's question is:

"Have you paid your rent today?"

Sunday, December 22, 2013

365QOD- Day1051

Wildly Successful

"What would make this (fill in the blank) wildly successful?"- Mike Williams, CEO of David Allen Co.

We often walk into situations. What I mean is that we walk into meetings, lunches, presentations, life events etc. where we just take part in the event. Majority of the time this is done without a plan.

The quote offers great wisdom. It makes sense to at least have a plan BUT to define what would make it wildly successful is genius. By defining the goal as being wildly successful we set ourselves up for a better experience.

Imagine starting a meeting and asking this question? Imagine asking your date what would make it wildly successful and just listening to the answer? In both situations you would be pleasantly surprised. The pause to ask the question of yourself and others will be worth gold. Try it!

Today's question is:
"What would make this (fill in the blank) wildly successful?"

Tuesday, December 31, 2013

365QOD- Day1060

Special Email

"Which reminds me... I had a very bright young woman in my office this week. She was bright and educated and clever and fantastic, but I have to admit, I wasn't buying her very well-expressed desire to join our team, so I said: Hey, look, I do career advice for a living. When you put the kids to sleep, and you have a moment in your day, and it's just you, what do you dream about doing?"-Marc Cenedella (in a 4th of July email)

How often do you save two year old emails? Or even better, do you re-read an old email from a stranger? Well, I have this old email from Marc Cenedella that he sent out couple of years ago and I have re-read the last two years. Why? Because the content resonates it reminds me of what is important.

The quote above helps to put me into the conversation between Marc and the person he is interviewing. The question asks the person as to what is important to them when the world no longer gets in their way. Wow! We often blame others and things for not getting to do what we need to do. But what about when there is nothing in your way, what do you dream of doing?

Today is the last day of 2013 and I believe we need to ask ourselves this very important question. It provides guidance as to what is truly important to us. Why is this important? Marc reminds us that:

"There's no storybook about "The Boy Who Followed Somebody Else's Dream", no movie rights sold for the tale of "It Wasn't Within My Purview To Consider Alternatives", no Sinatra tune entitled "I Did It The Way My Critics Requested I Do It"."

Today's question is:
"What do you dream about doing?"

Tuesday, January 7, 2014

365QOD- Day1067

Life Performance Review

"I am great!"- One employee's comment on their performance review form

At this time of year companies force their employees to do a self-evaluation of their performance. Their opinion hopefully matches the opinion of their supervisor. Either way it is stressful and seldom helpful.

But what I am talking about is an end of year review with yourself of yourself for yourself. You take a look at your performance across all areas of interest to you (work, family, financial, etc.) and review how well you did or did not do. Now that should be helpful.

I am a firm believer in stopping and thinking through our years. I have an underlining theme for the year (This year is The Year of the Sales) and I come up with 1-5 goals in each key area of my life. It is amazing to me but sometimes I do not even look at my list till the end of the year when I realize that many of the items have been achieved.

Today's question is:

"Have you ever given yourself a Life Performance Review?"

Thursday, January 9, 2014

365QOD- Day1069

ReMarkable

"What is the point of being alive if you don't at least try to do something remarkable?"- John Green

We all get one life. This quote brings home the idea of how important it is for us to do something meaningful with it. That part is the challenge

Unfortunately, most of our days are no different than the day before. We tend to live our lives as if tomorrow is guaranteed. For some reason we also believe the old age is guaranteed.

The wisdom in this quote is the word remarkable. The word remarkable to me means 'worthy of remark.' If no one comments on my post, is it remarkable? If no one takes the moment to think about it how it applies to them, is it remarkable? These are small ways I can test if my work is being noted or not. In the end if no one follows you or remarks about you, do you really contribute?

Today's question is:
"Was your day worth remarking about?"

Friday, January 17, 2014

365QOD- Day1077

You are the Average of Five People

"The best advice I ever got is: You're the average of the five people you associate with the most," Ferriss, author of the best-selling book "The 4-Hour Workweek the advice from a wrestling coach when he was in high school

I have heard this advice before but today I was reading a Business Insider story on best advice 12 successful entrepreneurs received and for some reason this one stopped me. My first thought was, "The advice is truthful but is it actionable?"

If I take the time and think about the 5 people, or most meaningful several people, in my life and ask myself, "What do these people average out to?" I can consider their income. Is my estimate of their income higher or lower than mine?

Another dimension I can consider is their overall happiness. Are their lives more fulfilling and happier than mine? Do they seem to exude happiness?

Overall balance is another dimension I should evaluate. Do they tend to spend their time working or living? Are they tied at the hip to their smart phone while spending time with the people in their lives? Do they take vacations to recharge?

I am sure there are other dimensions that you can come up with that might be more meaningful to you. The idea is powerful and very true. In the end you might decide that one or more of the people in your life are no longer aligned with what is important to you.

Today's question is:

"What are you and average of?"

Saturday, January 18, 2014

365QOD- Day1078

Becoming Above Average

"But I am not average."- a common belief that we all have

It is not uncommon to believe that we are better than the average. In yesterday post I discussed the idea that you are the average of five people you spend the most time in your life. I am sure that some, if not all, of you had a reaction to that idea.

So what does it really mean and how do you change it? Imagine a team of five members A, B, C, D, and F. Their values are 5, 4, 3, 2, and 1 respectively (5=excellent, 1=OK). You are the C. Why? Their average is sum/5= (5+4+3+2+1)/5=3 ==> C (you). **Any team will always have members that are better and below average.**

Now suppose everyone on the team raises their level by one. The average becomes (6+5+4+3+2)/5= 4. This is above average. **The lesson is if everyone improves the average gets better.**

Now what would happen if we drop the top team member (A) from the original team and replace the member with an average team member? The average becomes (3+4+3+2+1)/5=2.6 (slightly below average). And suppose everyone again raises their level by one. The new average becomes (4+5+4+3+2)/5=3.6 Not as good as the 4 before but pretty close. In other words even **replacing team members with average ones but the team strives for better you still come out better off.**

Consider would happen if we drop the bottom team member (A) from the original team and replace the member with an average team member. The average becomes (5+4+3+2+3)/5=17/5=3.4 (slightly above average). And suppose everyone again raises their level by one. The new average becomes (6+5+4+3+4)/5=4.2 Better than the original 4. In other words **replacing team members with below average scores and the team strives for better will make you the best team possible.**

Today's question is:
"How will you become better than average?"

Sunday, January 26, 2014
365QOD- Day1086

The Three Percent

"Can you drink a liter of water each day for thirty days?"- a question to an audience

The other day I watched a snippet from a seminar. In it the presenter explained to the audience that most of us are dehydrated. He then asked the audience if they could drink a liter of water for the next thirty days. The logic for thirty days was the old belief that if we do something for 21 days continuously it will become a habit. Everyone raised their hands agreeing that they would drink the liter of water.

The presenter then informed the audience when this experiment was done with 1000 people the result was that only 3% percent of the audience actually stayed committed to the end of the month. Shocking? I was expecting the three percent. It is no different than the number of people with written goals. The same number who actually persevere to achieve the great things with their lives.

So why did they fail? I believe that they committed intellectually. They know that drinking water is good for them and that the effect would be positive. As the Heath brothers would categorize it, the rider committed to the journey.

However, there was no emotional connection to the goal. Drinking water is not something that most of us get emotional about. Unless you have seen someone dehydrate in a matter of a couple of hours there is no emotional commitment. As the Heath brothers would categorize it, the elephant moved towards a different goal.

Even better there is no way to set you up on the path to getting to the one litter goal. It is not like pre-punching 2 holes on a reward card as Subway did. It is not like someone could have started you with one fourth of liter base level.

So the experiment is a set up for failure? Nope. In my opinion it is strictly willpower to commit and stay with that commitment. I urge you to set it as a goal and achieve it. Then raise the bar to 1.5 liters. I will commit to do so also.

Today's question is:
"Can you commit to drinking a liter of water for a month?"

Motivation

Friday, June 28, 2013

365QOD- Day875

"I would have more money, if I would have a plan" - Jim Rohn's response

When his mentor questioned the lack of plan, Jim responded with this little comeback. But then his mentor said, **"If you have a plan, then you would have the money."**

Why am I bringing this up? It seems to me that often we want A then B to happen But in reality it is B then A. It makes me wonder how often this is true.

A great example is whether action precedes motivation or does being motivated lead to action. I believe that we must act and that then motivation will come. It never works the other way around.

Today's question is:
"What is one if A then B scenario that you are accepting that you could be completely wrong about?"

Passion

Saturday, March 2, 2013

365QOD-Day756

"..secret creative life of others.."- Mel Resnof

The line above was another line I heard in the I Believe CD series. It immediately caught my ear and made me wonder.

Many of us have talents that if displayed would make the people around us marvel at why we are not pursuing that talent instead of working in our current job. Some people even take their secret talent to the grave.

I believe that many graveyards are full of dreams unfulfilled or delayed. We always believe that we will find the time to do it tomorrow. Tomorrow comes and we never seem to get to it.

We say that we did not have the time. BUT time never runs out. We run out.

Today's question is:
"What secret creative life you live that the world would benefit from?"

Saturday, May 25, 2013

365QOD- Day841

"My advice is to abandon the passion mindset which asks
    'What does this job offer me?
    Am I happy with this job?
    Is it giving me everything I want?'
Shift from that mindset to Steve Martin's mindset, which is ' What am I offering the world? How valuable am I? Am I really not that valuable? If I'm not that valuable, then I shouldn't expect things in my working life. How can I get better?" - Cal Newport

I have written about passion many of times in this blog. I am a firm believer that without passion we can get good results but never great ones.

This quote made me realize that the passion mindset is very self-oriented. Maybe Steve is correct?

In the end we would be more fulfilled if we satisfy the needs of others. By serving others we increase our value to the world. The greater the number of people that we serve, the greater our value to the world. I believe that they can be combined into a valuable passion mindset.

Today's question is:
" Do you have a valuable passion mindset?"

Sunday, May 26, 2013

365QOD- Day 842

"Building a moat: it takes time to dig the moat, but once established, it is nearly impossible to destroy." Steve Pavlina

The easiest way to think of a moat is the word advantage. Steve continues in a blog post:
" If you stick to your chosen field long enough, it gets harder to fail with each passing year:
1. More people will be aware of your existence than when you first started.
2. You'll have a bigger toolbox of strategies.
3. You'll have more clients and customers.
4. Your skills will increase.
5. You'll have more chances for fortunate opportunities to land on your plate.
6. And you'll be committing against people with increasingly less experience
than you have, relatively speaking."

I added the numbers for emphasis. This quote wonderfully illustrates the benefits of sticking with something for a long time. The advantages seem to outweigh the disadvantages.

Having worked in several industries I can tell you that the only disadvantage I can site is that you will be pigeonholed as that industry guy. When I left steel to go to academia I was asked why I wanted to do this.

When I left academia to go into consulting and running a business I was asked why I wanted to leave academia. When I left consulting and teaching to go back to industry I was asked why?

My moat is developing creative solution to problems.

To me what type of industry I apply it in is not important. What is important is the application of creativity to solving problems.

Today's question is:
" What is your moat?"

Wednesday, May 29, 2013

365QOD- Day845

"We do not need your restlessness or your excitement. We have enough Peter Pans, thank you very much. What we need is a little more conviction in our difference makers. We need your focus, your pluck, your courage. We need you to commit " - Jeff Goins

Many people are afraid of making a commitment. They are interested but do not want to commit.

Without the commitment, a team suffers. When the team members are not focused their efforts seem disjointed and not as effective.

As the quote points out too many of us have excitement but no conviction.

Today's question is:
"Are you committed to your work?"

Saturday, August 10, 2013

365QOD- Day917

This Sucks!

"What sucks in your world?" - Miki Agrawal Do Cool Sh$t book

I recently came across this author in the Entrepreneur magazine. The title of the book pulled me into her universe. So I had to look her up.

The question above was from a speech she delivered to the United Nations. She posed three questions of how to figure out what problem to solve. If the problem is making you miserable then most likely it is bothering others.

What also amazed me about her was how natural she was during an interview about her new book. She sat on a bed with so many off beat patterns but she pulled you into listening to her. Why? Because she was passionate about the topic. Her eyes sparked with energy. Her body could not sit still.

She was so passionate about her product that I ordered it. Her passion moved me towards action. I want to be as passionate about my products as she is about hers.

Today's question is:
"How passionate are you about your solution to the problem that sucks?"

Persistence

Wednesday, November 20, 2013

365QOD- Day1019

A Better Mousetrap

"Of all the myths of creativity, the Mousetrap Myth is perhaps the most stifling to innovation because it doesn't concern generating ideas. Rather, it affects how ideas are implemented. It's not enough for an organization to have creative people; it has to develop a culture that doesn't reject great ideas. It's not enough for people to learn how to be more creative; they also need to be persistent through the rejection they might face...We don't just need more great ideas; we need to spread the great ideas we already have." - David Burkus, The Myths of Creativity

The idea that if you come up with a better idea to do something that the world will immediately adapt is ludicrous. It just does not happen. The lone inventor developing a super complex idea is not unheard of but is rare.

I believe that most of us have many great million, if not billion, dollar ideas in our lifetimes. The problem is that these ideas only stay as ideas. They are just mental flossing and they never get to the intended customer as a product.

In industry it is even tougher to get an idea to get accepted and executed. Ideas need to be pushed through every layer of the organization. This is not an easy process and the pusher most often gets tired and gives up. The organizational culture has to be such to nurture those ideas (not reject them immediately) and give them nourishment to survive (funding).

As I mentioned in recent weeks I have become fascinated with the show Shark Tank. It seems kind of harsh when folks get rejected. But at least these are folks that took an idea and executed it. Some creations are more profitable than others and some people can sell the idea better to the venture capitalists (VCs). In the end they have a mousetrap that someone buys into.

There are many who get rejected by all of the VCs but immediately after walking out say that they still believe in their idea and that they will prove the VCs wrong. Some presenters even get contacted by other VCs who believe that they can help them. The key is the "they also need to be persistent through the rejection(s) they face…"

Today's question is:

"What better mousetrap will you persist though many rejections in order to execute?"

Thursday, January 2, 2014

365QOD- Day1062

Freedom to Fail

"Instead of trying to make your life perfect, give yourself the freedom to make it an adventure, and go ever upward"- Drew Houston, CEO of Dropbox

Humans are planners. I admit that I am one. I plan most things in my life BUT I truly enjoy when something unexpected happens. Life then turns into an adventure and it becomes memorable.

I believe that we do not like to fail and that is why we plan. We believe that by planning we can control our desired outcome. I believe that the planning process is very valuable but once you are into execution the plan often gets tossed. That does not make the planning process any less valuable. It gets you to think through the path before you have to adapt to the curves along the way.

Drew also said that,
"As you might expect, building Dropbox has been the most exciting, interesting and fulfilling experience of my life. What I haven't really shared is that it's also been the most humiliating, frustrating and painful experience too, and I can't even count the number of things that have gone wrong."

We need to hope that at end of execution that the experience turns out to be 'exciting, interesting and fulfilling.' BUT be ready for it to be 'humiliating, frustrating and painful experience' along the way. We have to detach ourselves from the outcome and put our best effort to make it a success. That is all that we can control.

As Einstein observed, **"God does not play dice with the world."**

Today's question is:
"Do you get discouraged by things going wrong along the way to success?"

PMP

Monday, December 23, 2013

365QOD- Day1052

People Pusher

"The project manager first has to be tough, second place has to be flexible. A motto I consider important is 'Never uncertain; always open.' I saw that in Latin (Numquam incertus; semper apertus) on the ceiling of a German fraternity in Heidelberg. It's important to always have a direction and be going there. You can't steer a ship that's not underway. But it's also important to be open to changes in circumstance and direction and not just to be completely bullheaded. A project manager also has to be a people person. Project management is a people function and most of the problems are people problems."- Fred Brooks author of the Mythical Man Month

I manage people and projects for a living. My goal is to always to get the project done ahead of schedule and under budget. There is science and art to getting this done.

The science part consists of having the knowledge of the project management framework that your organization follows. This is very different from one organization to another. Sometimes it is well spelled out in manuals and training. Other organizations do not follow a formal system and simply respond to the flow.

What Fred is talking about is the art piece. As he wisely tells us, most problems are people problems. You have to be tough to protect your organization's goal for the project but flexible enough with people to allow for reasonable changes. It is a fine line. The line, never uncertain, always open is the secret sauce.

Many project managers tend to fall into one or the other camp. I love both equally because I see them as complimentary and not as excluding the other. Just because I know the flow does not mean I can be effective in getting people to follow me. One without the other makes one a very incomplete project manager.

Today's question is:

"On your path are you certain but open?"

Receiving

Sunday, January 12, 2014

365QOD- Day1072

Delay vs. Deny

"God gives you answers in three ways: he says yes and gives you want you want, he says no and gives you something better, or he says wait and gives you the best."- Unknown

For many years I turned down every request that my kids made to me. No matter how medium or large size it was, I just told them no. Within a week or so I granted their request. Sometimes I even exceeded what they wanted in the first place.

This line teaches the principle behind my actions. We often want immediate gratification but life and God do not work in that fashion. Seldom do we immediately get what we want. BUT as my kids learned, the short wait is often worth it.

The principle behind the delay is the old marshmallow study in which kids were asked to deny themselves for 15 minutes when faced with a bowl of marshmallows. The ones who managed to deny themselves got twice as much candy vs. the tempted ones who immediately dug into them.

Today's question is:

"Could you delay your want to double your result?"

Result

Monday, January 6, 2014

365QOD- Day1066

Running Experiments

"I will do X and observe what happens to the output Y"- typical format of my experiments

A couple of months back I decided to label my posts. For the first 1000 posts I started them simply with the quote and decided to run an experiment. The experiment was to see if it made a difference to the number of readers if I simply added a title. The result is that it did increase the numbers by a little bit.

Today I did notice an unusual effect that I did not predict. I re-read just the titles of the last 60+ posts and found the flow between topics to be very interesting. But another observation was also disappointing. I do not believe that I create very effective hooks that pull in readers that might not know me really well. My understanding is that hooks should be like newspaper headlines begging you to buy the paper and read the story.

So try an experiment, observe the result on the number of readers, and then make another nudge. This is the main idea behind my first book, The Result, applied to blog audience.

Today's question is:
"Do you run experiments in your work?"

Routine

Monday, April 1, 2013

365QOD- Day786

"Why did I stop?" -my question to myself

While reading the book **The Tools** I learned that people that were helped with the tools will eventually go back to not using them. This immediately resonated with me.

I am always learning something new. But maybe it is too much? I do not always take the time to integrate it into my own system.

The only thing I can do is pause and capture my thoughts. It might jar me into using the tool.

Today's question is:
"How do you make yourself use helpful tools?"

Monday, April 15, 2013

365QOD- Day 800

"The mundane is to be cherished" - sign on The School of Life

While reading the February issue of Psychology I saw this sign on a building window. The article talked about how the school teaches life philosophy. The school is the idea of Alain D. Button.

I do believe that our lives are full of mundane tasks. These chores suck our energy dry.
That is only true if we let them.

If we take on the mundane by cherishing it then I believe we would see the beauty of the quote. If we can cherish it then it changes it into pleasurable.

Today's question is:
"Can you cherish the mundane?"

Friday, April 26, 2013

365QOD- Day811

"Good habits are hard to form but easy to live with, bad habits are easy to form but hard to live with" - Brian Tracy

I was listening to a marketing CD when this little gem was offered by Brian. I immediately saw the wisdom in the statement.

I am a firm believer of having or developing great routines. These routines eventually become so ingrained that they reach the habit level.

So I asked myself, "How does one create a habit?" Well, in my opinion start with a low expectation and design a routine. Since your expectation is low you give yourself the room to fail.

Every day presents the opportunity to follow your new routine. Make sure you monitor whether you follow it or you run the other way. By placing your focus on the routine and recording the success or failure of it, you will be more likely to succeed. Keep track of how often you fail and work on reducing the failure rate until you have a habit.

Today's question is:
" **How do you create a good habit?**"

Friday, May 10, 2013

365QOD- Day826

"We do know that fifty percent of the time people are online they're procrastinating. But we don't know whether, in fact, they wouldn't just use something else "- Timothy Pychyl

The thought of people wasting 50 percent of their time online is unbelievable. I mean I believe it but it just seems such a waste.

In the last six months I have been trying to do things more analog. I tend to sit at a desk that does not have a computer so I can think. I also trend to go to a lot of meetings in which I just bring a notebook and my cell phone. If I need to check email I can quickly do it on my phone but most of the time I just take notes in my Moleskin grid notebook.

For me this prevents me from sitting in front of a computer and potentially wasting time. I do believe that I can do better job at answering the mountain of email if I sit at the computer but maybe that is my next procrastination hurdle.

Today's question is:
"**How do you spend your surfing time?**"

Monday, May 27, 2013

365QOD- Day843

"While this is obvious in retrospect, a great way to free up your time to work on something new is to give something up. Instead of optimizing every second of your day (which is doable but very difficult to maintain), I believe the better option is to make a sacrifice"- Randall Degges

I have 168 hours each week. You have the same amount. We can try to squeeze in as much as we can but eventually it will become unsustainable.

Since we cannot make more hours then we have to figure out how to make better hours. By giving up some things that maybe have lost importance, we might gain enough time to pursue what is truly important to us.

Delaying a project is not the same a sacrificing. To me, sacrificing means to completely eliminate it from your future plans. That is the price for getting better hours.

Today's question is:
"**What is on your schedule that could be sacrificed?**"

Thursday, November 7, 2013

365QOD- Day1006

Restarting a Habit

"Why did I stop?"- My question to myself

Couple of weeks ago I created a weekly plan on Sunday. I then created daily time and energy plans. At the end of the day I marked off the items I accomplished. Amazingly, most of my items got done and I felt very productive. I felt like my days flowed better.

Which brings me to my question to myself. I know how well my system worked for me in the past. So why did I stop?

Why?

I kept asking myself this last weekend and the only reason I can come up with is that I focused on new things in my life instead. I know that since I did my time energy planning routine for an extended time it had created a habit. BUT just like I was able to create a habit I broke the habit.

What this experience taught me is that maybe I need to go back to some of the habits that were effective for me in the past that I have stopped doing. I need to review what worked for me before, test it if it is still effective, and if it is then re-teach myself the habit.

Today's question is:
"What old habit do you need to restart?"

Friday, November 8, 2013

365QOD- Day1007

Seven Days of Hell

"A phone for me is a tool, not a toy."-my words

My phone battery started not to charge fully about two weeks ago. So I started charging it more often. I even decided to buy a replacement battery. Hell, I bought three batteries and an external charger since I do not plan to change my phone for a few years.

Almost immediately after I had ordered the new batteries my phone went completely dead. I mean completely dead. It put me in a serious bind.

Currently I am using my phone a lot to practice for the PMP test. Also, while I drive to work and back I have been listening to past episodes of Shark Tank. So not only did my studying get distributed but my drive lost its purpose. It sucked!

I do not know about you, but this experience taught me how integral my phone is to my new routines. Without it my routines suffer and my productivity gets worse.

Interestingly, when I went on my month long hiatus last year and this year I did not miss my phone.

Maybe my expectation is that I would not use it much? So if I had to do without it during vacation it does not bother me much.

Today's question is:
"Which routines would get interrupted if you did not have a working phone for a week?"

Sunday, December 1, 2013

365QOD- Day1030

Nonrenewable Resource

"Time Filler=Time Waster"- a scary equation

We do not invest our 86400 daily gifts (24hrs*60min*60sec) as wisely as we should. It is not uncommon to check your email first as soon as you sit down at your desk. For most people this is a way of tuning into what is important.

I choose to start my day by walking and talking. Most often I get my coffee and walk over to see what people are working on and getting updated on what I need to do for them. This sometimes takes 15-60 minutes to accomplish.

Another big time waster is surfing the net. I have a rule. Every morning I go to my sources of information: Fast Company, Wired, 99u, entrepreneur, Inc., etc. and download a single article into a word document. I then print the packet and if I am tempted to surf, I just simply pick up the packet and start reading. This eliminates finding out what goofy stuff the world is reading about. If I want goofy stuff then simply just read the headlines on Yahoo.

Bottom line is that we need to look at the 86400 seconds as investments. We can throw them away or invest them into something that would help us become more of who we are and want to become.

We should always question. Scott Gerber offers these four questions to determine if an activity is worthwhile:"
1. Is the activity essential?
2. Is the timing right or would you be better served doing something else?
3. Is your presence absolutely necessary to complete the task?
4. Is there a better way to engage in this activity?"

And afterwards
"
1. Did the activity turn out to be the best use of your time?
2. Was adequate time allotted for the activity?
3. How could your time been spent more efficiently?
4. Will you participate in this activity again? If so, under what conditions?"

Today's question is:
"What are you investing your 86400 gifts (seconds) today?"

Sources

Thursday, February 14, 2013

365QOD- Day740

"Create a morgue file- file where you keep the dead things that you will later reanimate in your work"- Austin Kleone

I have a lot of boxes in storage. Due to space constraints I currently have only one box of my "stuff" with me. The stuff is ripped out pages from magazines, pictures, articles, notes, ideas, sketches, etc. These are contents of my 'morgue file'. Often they become a source for future projects.

Once in a while I go through the box and trim it into a slightly smaller version of the box. It never goes away because as I trim I also add to the box.

Sometimes I give myself the luxury of going through the file and just re-reading and getting myself inspired. As the author states, it reanimates me and my work.

Today's question is:
"Do you have a morgue file?"

Spiritual

Friday, April 19, 2013

365QOD- Day 804

"Could have been me."- My thought

I watched TV for the last couple of days and could not believe what was happening. The events in Boston pulled me in.

When I moved to Texas I started running local races. I ran in a couple of 10k and half marathons. My goal was to run the Chicago and New York marathons in 2012. Those were my training wheels before I attempted the most difficult Boston race.

If these events would have played out I would have been on Boston last Monday. Wow! What prevented me were the injuries along the way. Maybe they were blessings in disguise?

Today's question is:
"Do you understand how fortunate you are?"

Tuesday, April 30, 2013

365QOD- Day816

"But how?" - My former belief

Many years ago I sat at the end of the year on a beach in Florida writing out my goals for next year. One of the goals was how much I was going to make next year. This happened every year for three years in a row.

Looking back on those the years I made exactly what I wrote down. Did I do anything special? I am ashamed to say that I cannot remember specifically what I did to earn the extra but I did earn it.

Today I was listening to an audio book in which Brian Tracy described the same technique. He also said that he did not directly attribute it to anything the person does directly.

He recommended that each day we should write out our ten goals on a new page and ask ourselves what one action we could take towards the most important goal.

Today's question is:
" What ten goals would change your life completely if they came true this year?"

Saturday, May 18, 2013

365QOD- Day834

"Why the shape of a cross?"- A question asked by a priest during a sermon

Many years ago I attended a sermon that I will not forget as long as I live. The priest who gave the sermon asked this question. He proceeded to answer it.

He said that if you really started looking at the Ten Commandments you could summarize then into two:
1. **How man should behave towards men (he motioned side to side)**
2. **How man should behave towards God (He motioned from bottom up)**

The motions made the shape of a cross. I love his summary because many years later I remember the message.

Today's question is:
" **How are your relationships towards fellow men and God?"**

Sunday, August 18, 2013

365QOD- Day925

An Amazing Story

"This touched me."- My words

The other day I was going though and cleaning a bunch of old papers. I came across a story called Lunch with God. It is shown below:

A little boy wanted to meet God. He knew it was a long trip to where God lived, so he packed his suitcase with a bag of potato chips and a six-pack of root beer and started his journey.

When he had gone about three blocks, he met an old woman. She was sitting in the park, just staring at some pigeons. The boy sat down next to her and opened his suitcase. He was about to take a drink from his root beer when he noticed that the old lady looked hungry, so he offered her some chips. She gratefully accepted it and smiled at him.

Her smile was so pretty that the boy wanted to see it again, so he offered her a root beer. Again, she smiled at him. The boy was delighted! They sat there all afternoon eating and smiling, but they never said a word.

As twilight approached, the boy realized how tired he was and he got up to leave; but before he had gone more than a few steps, he turned around, ran back to the old woman, and gave her a hug. She gave him her biggest smile ever.

When the boy opened the door to his own house a short time later, his mother was surprised by the look of joy on his face. She asked him, "What did you do today that made you so happy?" He replied, "I had lunch with God." But before his mother could respond, he added, "You know what? She's got the most beautiful smile I've ever seen!"

Meanwhile, the old woman, also radiant with joy, returned to her home. Her son was stunned by the look of peace on her face and he asked, "Mother, what did you do today that made you so happy?" She replied! "I ate potato chips in the park with God." However, before her son responded, she added, "You know, he's much younger than I expected."

Too often we underestimate the power of a touch, a smile, a kind word, a listening ear, an honest compliment, or the smallest act of caring, all of which have the potential to turn a life around. People come into our lives for a reason, a season, or a lifetime! Embrace all equally!

Today's question is:
"Have you had lunch with God today?"

Monday, August 19, 2013

365QOD- Day926

There is a Reason

"The set up is just as important as the story."- Story telling advice

In post 925 I pasted the story called Lunch with God. I want to tell you an interesting story.

Three weeks ago I hurt my right knee. I went out for a short Sunday run and five minutes into the run my right knee just did not feel good. So I stopped. I thought it was my mind playing games so I tried again. No luck. Therefore I decided to give my knee a break and start using the elliptical machines in my building's fitness center.

For the last three weeks, my new routine stated with getting up at 430 in the morning and working out on the machine for an hour or so. Well, needless to say there is no one fighting you for these machines at 430. So I stated going down each day and playing my music on my phone and reading books.

The other day I had a surprise. I walked down to the center and there was a young guy about 12 looking at the machines. He was dressed in shorts, t shirt, and slippers. The guy did not look like he was in running shape.

He chose the machine next to me. We stated using the elliptically without saying a word. He smiled. I smiled.

A little later I turned my music playlist on. He just smiled. I also smiled.

For 75 minutes we both used the machines without saying a word.

The whole experience reminded me of the Lunch with God story. Mother Theresa used to say that she saw Jesus with his numerous disguises in all the faces she tended to during the day.

Who is to say that God just didn't want to work out that morning?

Today's question is:
"Have you ever worked out with God?"

Tuesday, August 27, 2013

365QOD- Day934

The Four Parts of Us

"The mind is the horses, the body is the chariot, the ego is the small child inside the chariot, and the spirit is the charioteer. Unfortunately most of the time the spirit is asleep and the horses are directing the chariot wherever they want to take it"-Naren Jauhal

The other day I had a conversation with Naren about our beliefs. We discussed the trinity idea of mind, body, and soul. But his idea was that there are four was new to me. Let's talk about it. The visualization is easy to see clearly.

I can see the little ego misleading the spirit into pursuing a self-centered goal. The kid is all about the need. Me, me and more me. It takes us away from or mission and drives us towards the selfish pursuit.

The chariot is the body. If it is strong it will follow whatever direction the spirit, the ego, or the mind sets for it. It is the follower. You ask it to run a mile it does. If you believe it can run ten miles then that is what it gives us. If you believe you cannot then it blocks you.

The horses are tied to the body. If the ego or spirit do not lead it then the mind takes over to lead it where it makes sense to it. Your body could be in great shape, but if your mind can tell you that there is something wrong with it the body believes it.

The last part is the spirit. If it is guiding the body-chariot, ignoring the ego-child, and raining in the mind-horses, it will lead them to the promised land-true destination.

Today's question is:
"Which one of the four leads you most often?"

Thursday, August 29, 2013

365QOD- Day936

Just a Fluke

"Coincidence is God's way of staying anonymous"- Emily Bear

When I read this line I laughed. Immediately I saw the truth hidden inside it. Just as fast I connected it to another belief.

The wisdom in the words is that the false belief that it is just a fluke is not correct. It is just simply God using coincidence to drive us towards a desired direction.

The belief that I have is something I read in a book called **Sacred Contacts**. In it the author Laura puts out the idea that before we are born we choose what we will experience in this life. God agrees to our plan but also asks of us to be in certain places at certain time and to influence certain people. Outside of those moments we are free to choose the life that we lead.

But maybe it is not that simple? Maybe we are guided all along by coincidences towards those moments. Some might say pushed towards them.

Today's question is:
"Did you feel God's anonymity on your back?"

Saturday, December 21, 2013

365QOD- Day1050

Hurting Others

"If you truly loved yourself, you could never hurt another."- Buddha

I do not intentionally hurt others. But... it does happen. I snap and without thought I say or do something that others perceive and feel as hurtful. This is where focused breathing helps to stop the blood from boiling.

The quote gives a very difficult task. To truly love oneself is very hard. We often talk the talk but fail to live up to that level. It must be that we do not feel "enough" and just take it out on the people around us.

Maybe we should reverse it and work on the second part of the quote first? Work on not purposely trying to hurt anyone and we might just get to the level of truly living ourselves. I think that most of us approach life and relationships in this fashion already. Judging by the amount of pain in the world, I do not believe it to be very effective.

So what is the answer? We have to remember that the Buddha left his wife and princely life in order to find himself. This seems selfish to most of us but maybe by being selfish and truly developing yourself one can evolve to this level of love for others.

Today's question is:

"Do you truly love yourself?"

Thursday, January 23, 2014

365QOD- Day1083

Of Service to Others

"Let me tell you a story"- My favorite words to hear

The other day I was driving home when I called a friend. James is a very good friend. He also happens to be very religious. At the end of our conversation he told me a story.

James told me a story how at work things were difficult. Nothing seems to gel. Everything seemed to lead to conflict with the people in his work environment.

Then one day he went to a sandwich shop. While in line he heard a voice instructing him to pay for the meal of the young couple in front of him. He ignored it. The voice inside came back a second and a third time. He could no longer ignore it, he offered, and paid for their meal. They were delighted and finally he was at peace.

According to James, the next day everything started changing. Life seemed to become easy and his relationships at work seemed to improve. It seemed as if someone had turned a switch on.

James' story made me realize that often we are self-focused too much. We are offered guidance from around us and above that we tend to ignore. But if we get out of ourselves then we will be rewarded with peace of mind and our lives will shift towards a better state.

Today's question is:

"Do you get out of yourself by being of service to others?"

Strategy

Thursday, April 25, 2013

365QOD- Day810

"Accountability buddy" - new idea to me

I recently ran across this label in a couple of places. This morning while getting rid of some old articles and looking for a source of inspiration for a post I ran into it again.

The Psychology article offered a suggestion by Stephanie Sarkis titled To Do 2.0
"Every morning, a friend and I text each other a list of tasks we need to get done that day. As we accomplish each task, we text to check in"

I immediately started thinking through my friend Rolodex in my mind as to who can be my accountability text buddy. Maybe try different people for a week? Maybe text each other the 1-3-5 daily list I wrote about in an earlier post?

Today's question is:
"Who is your accountability buddy?"

Wednesday, May 1, 2013

365QOD-Day817

"Can I have a minute of your time?" -common expression

I constantly work on several side projects. And often I hit a wall.

The wall is usually a lack of knowledge or expertise in a subject. Many times I do not even know who knows the answer.

While looking through Inc. magazine online stories it mentioned a site that offers access to experts such as Mark Cuban for a fee. His fee is 160 dollars per hour. Some experts offer their time free. Gary V. offers 15 minutes for free.

It makes me wonder how valuable the short time can be and how to best use the short time.

Today's question is:
" **What questions would you ask during a 15 minutes access to an expert?**"

Saturday, June 22, 2013

365QOD- Day869

"Bad strategy"- My observation

I love to watch NBA playoffs. This year's finals were especially interesting.

The two teams went back and forth winning games. In each game you can see the strategic changes they made to overcome the other team's strengths from previous games.

The last game came down to the last minute with each team having a chance at winning the championship. It was a nail biter. My choice, the Spurs, lost.

Why did they lose? Bad strategy. Even in a close game strategy is the difference maker.

One of the Spurs players, Green, was hot for most of the playoffs. He even set a record for most three point shots. So the team wanted him to be hot in game seven. It never happened. He had an off night. In first half of the game he missed ten shots.

So why am I writing about this? In my opinion a team needs to have a game strategy BUT be adaptive enough to recognize what is different this time vs. the past. The Spurs believed that Green would be hot but he wasn't. They believed that James could not hit three point shots when he is not contested. He did 4 in a row. They believed that Wade could not hit jumpers. He did.

The Spurs needed a trigger for their strategy. If Green misses 5 on a row, take him out. If James his three in a row, put a hand in his face. And so on.

Darwin never said that the strongest survive. Spurs were the stronger and deeper team. He did say that the most adaptive survive. Miami Heat was more adaptive. They won.

Today's question is:
" Do you use triggers to force you to be more adaptive?"

Saturday, September 21, 2013

365QOD- Day959

How many knives does a chef need?

"Last year I believed that these five exercises are all one needs, but this year I have added three more"-Dragan Stojmanovich

Last year Dragan shared his five exercises with me. Full of energy he could not sit still without showing them to me. He told me that those five exercises were all you will ever need to keep in great shape.

This year he told me that he added three more because he was saw them and quickly realized the benefits. Now his exercise set consists of eight exercises.

This encounter made me think about the minimum set of tools needed to accomplish a job. Maybe it is five or eight or just one? And what will make you realize that you need to add a tool?

I believe that we always have to examine what we do and think about how to do it better. This awareness will lead us to realizing that we are missing a tool. Or if we are not using a tool to get rid of it.

Today's question is:
" **How do know when you have the right amount of tools for the job?**"

Friday, September 27, 2013

365QOD- Day965

The Disconnect

"I know that I should eat healthy and I don't. I know that I should spend time with my kids and I don't. I know that money, yes, will not make me happy and I am still keep trying to make money. It is an amazing thing about humans that we have these mistakes that we make all the time and it is not lack of information." Michael Nortonon Harvard professor

I believe that I know a lot on many topics. Man I can reach into my brain and extract information on what I should be doing. But as the quote teaches we know what we should do but we still do not.

The key word is information. He says that we have a lot of information. What that means to me is that we had a lot of data we were exposed to and we converted that data into information. So where do we fail?

In previous posts I talked about the idea of going from data to information to knowledge to wisdom. As we know, just by having information does not guarantee that we will do what we have information on. We are only half way on our journey towards wisdom.

Notice that the quote also uses the word 'know' repeatedly. This implies the presence of knowledge. So that will place us three quarters of the way on our path to wisdom.

The failure then is going from knowing to wisdom. I believe that knowledge is the how and the wisdom is the why. If the why we do something is not greater than the how then the gap exists and we are more likely to fail.

Today's question is:
"How do you make your why greater than your how?"

Saturday, September 28, 2013

365QOD- Day966

Stop Rounding

"Use a more precise anchor in negotiating"-negotiating advice

I have a tendency of rounding numbers up. When approximating I always give myself a little bit of wiggle room. What can it hurt?

Well consider a scenario in which you are interviewing for a job and everything goes well. The company offers a round number as your new salary. You counter with a more precise number that does not include zeroes. Immediately you stand out as having done your homework. The conversation continues.

Consider developing a budget for a large project. You study your estimates and round up the numbers to give yourself the wiggle room. When you present your numbers they do not look precise enough and they are immediately challenged because they look too perfect.

Moral of this post is that we must use a more precise anchor numbers in order to improve our chances of negotiating success.

Today's strategy is:
"Can you stop rounding your estimates?"

Thursday, October 17, 2013

365QOD- Day985

Nurture vs. Nature

" The old debate."- My thought

On post 984 I talked about two different ways of presenting information. My conclusion was that they were both correct.

So what about this question of nature vs. nurture? In another post I talked about my three books. I have created what I believe are three wonderful books. That is the nature part.

But I seriously lack the nurturing part. I do minimal social media marketing. After I publish I post them on my Facebook and Twitter pages. But that is it. And based on the sales, it is not enough.

My advice yesterday was that we need to train ourselves in one type of presentation and then expand to the second type in order to become more complete. The same advice follows for me, now that I have learned the nature portion- how to create and publish, I need to spend some time learning and doing the Nurturing.

Today's question is:
"How do you know it is time to move away from Nature and move into Nurture of an idea?"

Thursday, October 31, 2013

365QOD- Day999

Bigger Problems

"Don't wish it were easier, wish you were better. Don't wish for fewer problems, wish for more skills. Don't wish for less challenge, wish for more wisdom."-Earl Shoaff

In several previous posts I have talked about the idea of not wishing your problems to go away. The same thing can be said about complex people in your life.

The quote reminds us that we should strive to be better, more skillful, and wiser than our problems. I completely agree. By being more our problems will seem smaller and could be managed.

Problems never go away. They morph into different problems or more difficult version of the same problem. By being in the now and focusing yourself on solving it you guarantee that you will know how to solve it in the future. This moves you up to bigger and more challenging problems. Before you say that you don't want that, remind yourself that bigger problems = bigger $$$.

I wish you bigger problems in your life.

Today's question is:
"What are you truly wishing for at this moment?"

Thursday, November 14, 2013

365QOD- Day1013

Parkinson's Law

"Work expands as to fill the time available for its completion"- Cyril Parkinson

I agree that a task will swell to fill the time. I also believe that this is true mostly because of: believed complexity, perceived difficulty, and upon the amount of time that you allocate to the task. Let's drill down into these.

Complexity is interesting. When I say complexity what I am saying is something that might not be very difficult but requires many steps to complete. If it requires you to do 20 steps to get to the end, the goal is complex because you have to go through 20 hurdles to get it done. Each one of the steps might be quick and easy but without all 20 the task most likely will not get completed.

Similarly, perceived difficulty is in the eye of the beholder. If I believe that something is difficult for me to accomplish then I have already created a wall I have to really want to jump over. However, just because I believe it to be difficult does not make it difficult for others. There are adults that do not know how to ride a bike. They believe it to be difficult. The rest of us do not.

I can see the wisdom in Parkinson's statement. Work will expand to fill the time available. Sometimes complexity or level of difficulty is not even an issue. If I get up early and have three hours to kill before I have to leave home then guess what? I will find something to fill those three hours. It might not be very productive but it will fill the time available.

Today's question is:

"What can you do not to fall into Parkinson's trap?"

Saturday, November 16, 2013

365QOD- Day1015

Plan the Journey NOT the Goal

"Is the goal more important than the journey?"- A philosophical question

I tend to be a goal oriented person. When a goal is important to me, I identify what the goal(G) is and then break it down into objectives(O), consider multiple strategies(S) to achieve each objective, plan(P) the proper sequence through the objectives and which strategies to use, while assigning a daily action(A) and paying attention to the learnings(L). This is my version GOSPAL version of Bryan Tracy's GOSPA technique.

While reading 99U posts I notices this blurb by James Clear from iDoneThis:
"Instead of giving yourself a deadline to accomplish a goal and then feeling like a failure if you don't achieve it, you should choose a goal that is important to you and then set a schedule to work towards it consistently. That might not sound like a big shift, but it is."

The L in gospaL is intended to make one realize to pay attention to the progress and to be wise enough to make adjustments. The P in gosPal is the planning of the sequence and scheduling of the tasks. I often use a 3 month window to fight through a worthwhile goal. The A in gospAl is where the schedule is broken down on the individual tasks that need to get done in order to reach the ultimate G.

With this bit of breakdown, I conclude that James is correct and that my goal achieving procedure contains his idea of focusing on the schedule and the journey not the big goal. This allows me to focus on the tasks instead of feeling overwhelmed at the size of the goal.

Today's question is:

"Do you focus on the journey schedule or on the goal?"

Monday, November 18, 2013

365QOD- Day1017

Predicting the Future

"I wish that I was more productive"- a common desire

This weekend I read a story called **A smartphone app that predicts future to-do list tasks**. The company which produces the app is 24me. It is one of the highest reviewed and popular apps at iTunes. I checked immediately and there is not an android equivalent.

What attracted me to the app is that "its creators say can predict future items on a user's daily to do list." It is in a sense according to them a "long-term personal assistant". This is all done through Artificial Intelligence and access to your calendar and social accounts.

So why did I think this is cool? I am eventually going to publish a book that teaches how to manage time and energy. Managing time is just one aspect. Managing time and energy together is where the magic occurs. To me, creating an app that teaches my system is a future goal. I never thought about adding the complexity of AI to improve the time management.

I believe that this idea will improve the calendar feature by collecting information from different social accounts but it will not help one get a balance. For that you need my app. LOL!

Today's question is:

"Is having a way of pulling information from social sites into your calendar desirable to you?"

Thursday, December 5, 2013

365QOD- Day1034

Having no Regrets

"It gets easier every day to project a future without regret; to be the best, most optimal people we can be today, so that we can look back without ambivalence. Life is not mysterious, it's mathematics. All we have to do is track our productivity, our spending, our steps, and our calorie intake. All we have to do is count our friends and likes and follows. The illusion of control that these tools grant us over every aspect of our lives is powerful. There is always something we can do today to avoid regret tomorrow. To admit regret is to admit to a previous failure of self-control." Carina Chocano, Aeon Magazine

Wow! What a quote! Let us tear it apart.

As the quote teaches, life is not mysterious and it is simply mathematics. For most part, I would agree with Carina. I do belief that if we can account for all of the inputs and understand the system, then we can predict most future events.

Carina's guidance is to have systems that we use to track our lives. These could be paper or electronic. You will definitely have information. BUT as Carina says, it is an illusion of control. There is a bit of unpredictability that we will never be able to account for.

However, if we track our lives then we will have less regrets tomorrow. This makes sense to me. The failure to plan, track, execute will lead to regrets mostly because we did not exercise "self-control."

Today's question is:
"Do the things you regret about your life stem from lack of self-control?"

Saturday, January 4, 2014

365QOD- Day1064

Intermediate Steps

"What is your intermediate step?"- My question

Recently I talked with a person who was so focused on their goal that when I asked this question they looked stunned. Their response was, "Why is that important?" I almost fell over out of my chair.

I believe that identifying our end goal is very important. BUT you can lose the war if you do not fight the small battles along the way. To me the intermediate goals are the key. These smaller objectives let you keep your forward momentum towards the goal.

When I asked this question I asked the person, for his goal, I was looking for him to identify one large intermediate step. I do believe that a bunch of smaller steps is better than one big step but not always. Sometimes one large intermediate objective is better. When?

Consider someone interested in going to medical school. She is still in high school and believes that being a doctor is her calling. She is applying to different schools to get a basic science degree as the intermediate step. But getting a basic science degree gets her almost nothing. Those degrees are OK but do not provide a great intermediate step because they do not lead to great paying jobs.

What would happen if she would pursue a pharmacy degree? She will walk out as a doctor of pharmacy within 6 years instead of 4. BUT now you are a doctor already. If you want to pursue an MD degree then the world is yours. If you chose to continue towards the MD you can. If you decide that you had enough of school you can get a great paying job.

The point is that a great intermediate step could also be a great stopping point if need be.

Today's question:

"Does a great intermediate step exist on your journey to your goal?"

Tuesday, January 14, 2014

365QOD- Day1074

Tools Can Make You or Break You

"Computers are only amplifiers. They can amplify your intelligence or amplify your stupidity. Which would you like?" -- Richard Campbell

I believe that this quote can easily be re-written and more relevant as: **"Smart phones are only amplifiers. They can amplify your intelligence or amplify your stupidity. Which would you like?"**

Most people would probably rather lose $100 rather than lose their smart phone. They become an amplifier for what we do every day. I know for me my smart phone is a tool.

What I like about this quote is that it instructs that they can be used to amplify one's intelligence or one's stupidity. If I am playing games mindlessly then I am leaning towards stupidity. If I am analyzing an app and later create a better app then the phone is amplifying my intelligence. Outlining a book is intelligence but reading mindless novels is fun but not very productive.

So chose your tools carefully and even better how you use them wisely.

Today's question is:

"Which one are you amplifying?"

Tuesday, February 4, 2014

365QOD- Day1094

Becoming an Attractive Person

"Magic mirror in my hand, who is the fairest in the land?"- The evil queen

This post has nothing to do with beauty. It does have to do with being more attractive. What I am talking about is becoming attractive in the sense of having more opportunities that come into your life.

Most of us can relate to the concept of dating. I am sure that most of us have gone through periods of our adult lives when we were not dating anyone but wanted to. In my opinion the worst thing that one can do is force things. You can put yourself in situations where you believe a potential mate can be found. Going to a bar to find someone is a foolish strategy. It is hard to stand out.

I believe that doing a search this way is foolish strategy. In my life I have always followed an alternate strategy. I believe that during those periods when doing a search the best that I can do is to work on myself. This was something I can control. I could not control whether someone found me attractive. Unbelievable as it may seem, when I followed this strategy I immediately was found.

This strategy can also be used when looking for a job opportunity. Unlike many, I do not believe in applying to many jobs. The result that we would wish for cannot be controlled by applying for many jobs. But improving what is on your resume is something you can control. With LinkedIn it is even easier for this strategy to work. Many recruiters all looking through profiles for that attractive person to fit a role that they need to fill. If you improve your profile, recruiters will find you more attractive.

Today's question is:

"What would make you more attractive?"

Stretching

Thursday, May 2, 2013

365QOD- Day 818

"Another number story" - my observation

I cannot help but notice that there are many stories that start with a number. 5 ways to become your best, 10 ways to be more productive, etc.

In my opinion, someone had figured out that a leading number catches the attention of readers. So now they use it and use it and use it.

It makes me wonder when an effective technique gets old? If you are getting results then you probably do not care but over time less and less people will read your stories.

Today's question is:
" **How do you decide when you need to get a new method for getting a result?**"

Saturday, February 16, 2013

365QOD- Day742

"One of the most profound lessons I've learned is that life we don't go through things; we grow through them"- Mo'Nique

Wow! I love this quote. The way I say the same thing is not as short and sweet as Mo'Nique's quote.

I believe we all are at a level in handling different issues that come up in our lives. So if I am a level 5 person then a level 7 problem seems impossible to solve.

So what happens then?

Most often we just simply wish the problem to go away. BUT I believe the wisdom is that we must raise our level to be above 7 in order to easily handle the problem.

As the quote points out 'we must grow through them' in order to handle things.

Today's question is:
"How do you grow through your problems?"

Tuesday, February 26, 2013

365QOD- Day752

"Oh, to be young, and an entrepreneur"- USA TODAY story caption

This story made me think. What is changing?

"According to a Gallup Poll released in January 43% of students in grades five-12 want to be entrepreneurs, and around the country youngsters are signing up for lessons in business savvy. Almost 60% say their school has classes on how to start a business, up from 50% in 2011. Those numbers don't even include after school entrepreneur workshops"- Oliver St. John in USA TODAY story

I believe that, just like many adults have become disappointed by Wall street, kids are being proactive. They would rather create something for themselves rather than depend on some large business for their security.

God bless them! I think our country will be better off with more people thinking like entrepreneurs than employees. (In the long run this will reduce the ability to outsource a person's work.)

I believe that the street goes both ways. An employee can become an entrepreneur. An entrepreneur might not succeed and go back to being an employee. However, after being an entrepreneur the person will never be the same. They might decide to be an "intra-preneur" within a company instead of just being an employee. Their world has been stretched as an entrepreneur and can never be the same employee.

Today's question is:
"How secure are you being an employee?"

Sunday, March 31, 2013

365QOD- Day785

"You are going to teach what?" - A co-worker's surprise

The other day I was asked to teach a yoga class. Yup! Did I care if I made a fool of myself? Could I fail?

When confronted with choices in life, I believe that we always ask ourselves one very important question. It is "Why me?" or "Why not me?"

I tend to look at my world from the why not me perspective. Steve Jobs' words to the Stanford class to stay young and stay foolish resonate with me. If there is no room for failure then there is no room for growth. By stretching one grows.

The only question of the two that stretches you is, **"Why not me?"**

Today's question is:
"What have you done lately that scares you?"

Sunday, April 14, 2013

365QOD- Day799

"If you see different things, you will see differently" - Robert Trajkovski

Every day you brush your teeth with your dominant hand. Have you ever tried to brush them with the other hand? Probably it did not feel natural and you switched back.

When I write the posts for this blog I typically write them on a computer. But lately I have been writing them on my phone. It had been a change that I now welcome. It forces me to read the posts more closely.

No it did not feel as natural as sitting in front of a computer. I could not figure out how to do certain things but with time and effort I believe that it will become a true alternative.

Today's question is:
"What feels totally unnatural to you but might be a great alternative if mastered?"

Wednesday, May 8, 2013

365QOD- Day824

"Take a bite...go on" - an urging

In life, we are often presented with many opportunities. These opportunities offer growth and adventure. Some are traps presented as opportunities.

However, just because the opportunity for adventure is in front of us we might not take it. And when we do, it might be too late. We might be afraid of what we discover or who we become!

Not pursuing the adventure leads us to discover less, achieve less, create less, etc. In the end we live a lesser life.

Today's question is:
" **What pulls you towards adventure instead of away from it?**"

Monday, June 17, 2013

365QOD-Day864

"What happens after the 'I did it' moment?"- Joshua Davis

After experiencing great success Joshua became uninspired. The way he described it at 99u conference speech is, **"That moment of being amazed by the unknown had left me."**

Joshua felt the **"sluggishness of the comfortable"**. In my opinion this is a very dangerous place to be.

A few years ago, during a meeting I uttered the words, "When you feel comfortable, it is time to get uncomfortable." My then boss loved it and stated quoting it in larger meetings.

I happen to work in a chemical plant. Getting comfortable in a chemical plant is just plain stupid. It is like working on a time bomb. It is not whether if it will go off, it is a matter of when it will go off. We have a lot of procedures that force us to ask tough questions of ourselves when making changes. Amazingly, even with all those procedures things always get missed.

Today's question is:
" How do you overcome the sluggishness of bring comfortable?"

Saturday, June 29, 2013

365QOD- Day876

"Be confident and take risks, because if you're not going to, someone else is."-Zach Schau
Pure fix cycles

One of the labels that I use in my blog is the "I am" label. In it I discuss the words for each letter that I say out loud to myself. The B word that I want to be more of is Bold.

The quote above is another way to define bold. To me it says, either you do it or someone else will be bold to take action. Although, in the quote action is called risk.

I believe that we all take risks. For most of us we tend to want to reduce risk and just survive. It is within our prehistoric nature to want to reduce risk and that we minimize it to the point that we guarantee our survival.

But this risk avoidance is risky. It does not improve us or stretches us to new territory. This risk avoidance limits our success potential. Another way to say it is, **"No risk= No reward"**

Today's question is:
"Are you bold enough to increase your risk level? "

Monday, December 30, 2013

365QOD- Day1059

New Resolution

"I will stop adding sugar to my coffee and tea."- My last year resolution

Last year I decided to stop adding sugar to my coffee and tea. I had read many studies that reported that just by stopping pop drinking you could lose 12 pounds. It made sense so I decided to do a small experiment on myself. I stopped for a year.

So what happened? I managed to not add sugar directly to my coffee or tea for a year. This may not seem like much BUT to me, before making this decision, it was impossible. Impressive?

Well, I think anytime we manage to improve anything about ourselves we should pat ourselves on the back and gloat. I am. But the drawback of the experiment was that it did not change my weight very much. My weight tends to oscillate between 215 and 225. If I exercise more it tends to be towards 215 and if I tend to overeat it leans towards 225. Adding sugar made no difference.

To me what is important is that I do not miss the sugar. Now I actually prefer the taste of my coffee black because I finally taste the coffee and not the cream, milk, or sugar. Simply, I just taste the quality of the coffee.

Since it is the end of the year I have been thinking about what I want to get rid of in 2014. It is only a day away and after some serious thought I have decided to give up my favorite vice- chocolate. I will not eat any desert during the next year. What this means is that I have a lot of chocolate cleaning in my office to do tomorrow…LOL

Why chocolate? I decided that even though I removed adding sugar I did not eliminate it totally from my diet because I still kept eating chocolate and deserts and once in a while drinking a pop. Man this is going to be tough! I will attempt to eliminate chocolate, deserts, and pop for a year.

Today's question is:

"Could you give up your first and second favorite vices?"

Success

Saturday, July 13, 2013

365QOD- Day890

"Success = Mindset + Skillset+ Get off your Assets "- James Malichak

This equation is made up of three components. According to James they are all important in order for one to experience success. Let's break them down.

What we think and how we think makes up our mindset. It is the setting of our mind to do something or not do it. Without the correct mindset we might do the wrong things.

Skillset is whether we know how to do the things we want to accomplish. If there is an ability gap then we have to be wise enough to find the training and be willing to take advantage of it to shrink the gap.

The success magic only occurs once the third component is present. We can sit on our assets and think and think but that does not make things happen. Thinking for planning pauses is important but you still have to take action on your plan.

In my opinion, success is based on the following percentages: the get off your assets is 60%, 20% for mindset, and 20% for skillset. The biggest key is the get off your assets portion.

Today's question is:
"How do you make yourself get off your assets?"

Monday, April 8, 2013

365QOD- Day793

"...Assume that on any given day you can accomplish one big mission, three medium tasks, and five small things. Get those done as best as you can. Then, as your workday concludes make the next day's 1-3-5" Alex Cavaulacos, Muse

This advice is perfect for a crazy busy culture that we live in. Place the big mission in front of you, THEN tackle the tasks AND lastly the things.

I remember seeing this done in an experiment with a big vase with big, medium, and small balls. The same idea as the quote but then we were asked if anything else would fit. We added sand. Lastly we added water.

It is amazing what you can squeeze in a day when the big pieces go in first, followed by medium, etc.

Today's question is:
"How do you squeeze in your 1-3-5?"

Thursday, April 18, 2013

365QOD- Day 803

"Talent is like a sundial in the shade"- Ben Franklin

The other day while driving I heard this quote. How useful is a sundial in a shade? Not useful at all.

We all possess talents that make doing certain things easier. We look magical to others when we are doing those things, because they might not have the same talent. Their talent might impress us just like our talents impress them.

The message to me is that the talents have to be displayed in the right setting for them to be useful. If they are, then they make us look like we are doing something magical.

Today's question is:
"How do you align your talents in your life?"

Tuesday, April 23, 2013

365QOD- Day 808

"Inspiration is useless without perspiration" - Anonymous

I recently spent some time getting rid of old papers. While re-reading some articles I came across an old HBR article by John Baldoni with this quote.

I believe that I get inspired by many things that I read. At times I might even get a piece of paper and start sketching my new derived idea down.

But, as the quote advises, it is useless without the perspiration. I must be willing to work with and on the idea in order to make something of it. Spending a little bit of time thinking and sketching is not enough. The gods require sweat.

Today's question is:
" **Are you sweating or are you simply thinking?**"

Thursday, July 11, 2013

365QOD- Day 888

"Ability is what you are capable of doing. Motivation determines what you do. Attitude determines how well you do it."-Lou Holtz

This was a quote on a wall in my first office. I recently found it and stopped to think about it. Quickly I realized that all three are important. Why?

Without ability or the plan to develop your capabilities you will not do the things you want to do. It takes wisdom and willingness to take a look at yourself and understand what you are capable of and what are your gaps that need closing.

Without motivation we tend to not want to move forward. The biggest secret to motivation is to do something small towards your goal. Amazingly that little motion will motivate you to take the next small step.

The last piece is the attitude. If you are unsure of your abilities or feel lack of motivation you will not have the best attitude to strive forward. You have to believe you can and be willing to take the small step. The last ingredient is the secret sauce. Without the best 'I can' attitude you will not succeed even if you have the ability and motivation.

Today's question is:
"How would you rate your ability, motivation, and attitude in your current endeavor?
(on a scale of 1 worst to 10 best) "

Imho you need at least a score of 27 to succeed.

Saturday, September 7, 2013

365QOD- Day945

Think

"1. How You Think is Everything: Always be positive. Think success, not failure. Beware of a negative environment"-IBD first of ten secrets to success

Investor's Business Daily is a daily newspaper that I used to subscribe to in the past. In the next ten posts I will give my opinions and stories on the ten traits that IBD spent years analyzing leaders and successful people in all walks of life to collect. IBD believes that these traits can turn dreams into reality.

Many books on success focus on psychology of thought. If a person is against themselves then there is no need for negative outside forces to keep the person down. However, a positive person will always come out better off than someone who thinks that the world conspires against them.

As Henry Ford used to say, "If you think you can, or you think you can't, you are right." This positive belief that you can is the seed needed to succeed. It however had to be nurtured.

Nurturing provides the nutrients that accelerates the growth. If the environment is full of people pulling you down, it will be harder for you to rise above. In an old post I told the story of five monkeys. It is a wise parable that teaches us how powerful environments are in forcing us into believing anything, no matter how wrong it is.

So learn to think for yourself. Surround yourself with positive people and environments that nurture and support you in your dreams. In my opinion, 20% of your time should be spent thinking about what you should be executing in the present and the future.

Today's question is:
"Do you spend 20% of your time thinking quality thoughts?

Sunday, September 8, 2013

365QOD- Day946

Decide

"2. Decide Upon Your True Dreams And Goals: Write down your specific goals and develop a plan to reach them."-IBD second of ten secrets to success

Making decisions is a part of life. We struggle with the small ones and typically postpone the big ones. But let us think through this quote.

The advice is to decide your true dreams and goals. Thinking can only be done by you with a lot of time and paper. Put it down, modify it over time, and change what parts lose importance.

You are allowed to change over time. Don't expect your dreams to stay the same. It would be silly if only your dreams as a ten year old were your only true dreams and goals. Write them down, put dates, and write in different colors to signify changes or deletions.

After you have thought through them, then lay out plans on how you would achieve them. I reference you to a series of posts I write on the GOSPAL technique. It will walk you from the goal, to objectives, through strategies, developing plans, creating daily actions, and capturing what you learned. Achieving goals is a unique endeavor that should be time bound and has the possibility of failure. If there is no potential to fail then the dream is not big enough.

Make sure that whatever you decide are your true dreams pull you towards their accomplishment. If someone has to make you do a task towards your goal then it is not truly your goal.

Today's question is:
"What are your true dreams and goals?"

Monday, September 9, 2013

365QOD- Day947

Action

"3. Take Action: Goals are nothing without action. Don't be afraid to get started now. Just do it."-IBD third of ten secrets to success

As I mentioned in yesterday's post, the GOSPAL technique is great for goal achieving. Notice that the first four letters are all about dreaming, thinking, and planning. It is the fifth letter that begins the action process to get something done.

As the quote cautions, goals are nothing without action. It is only mental masturbation. It makes you feel good but has no useful product.

The quote also encourages us not to be afraid. Just do it now. Don't wait till tomorrow to do something towards your goal. The size of the move does not matter but the direction is vital.

Today's question is:
"What are you just going to do now?"

Tuesday, September 10, 2013

365QOD- Day948

Learn

"4. Never Stop Learning: Go back to school or read books. Get training and acquire skills."- IBD second of ten secrets to success

This bit of advice fits me perfectly at the moment. A few months ago I concluded that I need to attend some formal training. I have the ability to self-teach myself anything but I realized that I need to put on my white belt on and become the student.

Since I made that decision I have attended a six sigma green belt for two weeks. I also attended a week long PMP test prep course. I enjoyed the hell out of them!

It is my belief that we have to constantly review our skill gaps and develop a plan to fill them. We are lucky now that with the internet learning something new is just a few clicks and videos away.

In my opinion we should have at least one book we are working through every week. Force yourself to complete it and then spend time thinking about it. What is still not clear? What could use a bit more work?

Today's question is:
"How do you keep yourself learning?"

Wednesday, September 11, 2013

365QOD- Day949

Persistent

"5. Be Persistent And Work Hard: Success is a marathon, not sprint. Never give up."-IBD fifth of ten secrets to success

Persistent is one of my twenty six power words. It is a wonderful word and its power grows exponentially when coupled with hard work. Why?

First of all, we can persist in the wrong things. So once we are working on true dreams and goals, we have to expect to put in hard work. Remember by definition our dreams have to be daring enough that we can fail. This makes them something we will have to work hard to achieve.

As Churchill wisely advised, **"Never. Ever. Never ever give up!"** To me that is the ultimate persistence.

Once you make the decision that something is important enough for you to persist, then do not ever give up. Expect the process to be a marathon. When I run half marathons, my mindset is different than when I go out for a five kilometer jog. I have to be willing to persist even when the body might decide to quit. I only stop if my body hurts not if it only complains.

Today's question is:
"How do you know you are being persistent enough?"

Thursday, September 12, 2013

365QOD- Day950

Analyze

"**6. Learn To Analyze Details**: Get all the facts, all the input. Learn from your mistakes."-IBD sixth of ten secrets to success

As the old sayings goes, "The devil is in the details." It is the understanding of details that allows one to be comfortable with making hard decisions. This only happens with analysis.

When I analyze a problem, I often ask myself if I understand all of the inputs and outputs. It is easy to simplify and miss a critical input. Without that input we might not have a clue as to why a system produces a particular output.

It is kind of like trying to find the cause of why a kid is doing poorly in school by only blaming the kid. It is a complex system. We have to look at the school, the habits, the teachers, the parents, the environment, the friends, etc.

The last part of the advice is to learn from mistakes. I think I am going to start a notebook called My Favorite Daily Mistake. I think by ripping my mistakes apart it will teach me how not to repeat it and to improve the quality of mistakes I do make.

Today's question is:
"What strategy do you use to analyze details?"

Friday, September 13, 2013

365QOD- Day951

Focus

"7. Focus Your Time And Money. Don't let other people and things distract you."-IBD seventh of ten secrets to success

I have been blessed with great examples of people around me who have great focus. My daughter has what I call scary focus. My wife has what I call laser focus.

Scary and laser focus are my ways of explaining how focused they are in not allowing other people and things from distracting them. They focus so tightly on the goal that you cannot see the target glow. It is just the pin point dot that shows up.

I am more of a broad point. You can see the direction but the total focus point is not very clear. As a matter of fact you might have to look on another wall to find it. I allow disturbances to take me away from my task. Maybe this is a fault that I need to control? Now that I know it is a desirable trait maybe I should manage it better.

Today's question is:
"Where do you focus your time and money?"

Saturday, September 14, 2013

365QOD- Day952

Be Different

"8. Don't Be Afraid To Innovate; Be Different: Following the herd is a sure way to mediocrity."- IBD eighth of ten secrets to success

This is so me. I have never fit a mold. I might borrow a term from Naren and call myself a maverick. I never truly fit the boxes I am put in.

During my working career I have had many titles but I might just call myself a problem solver for my company. Often I look at what is required from me and try to understand what the problem truly is that I am being asked to solve.

I never stop there. Just because it is someone else's problem it does not mean that it is cool to me. So I ask myself, what is it the problem that I could solve that is cool to me and whose subset will provide a solution for my company.

Believe me when I tell you, solving a cool problem will excite you and move you forward more than just solving others peoples' problems. This innovation can get you promoted faster and result in larger pay raises.

Today's question is:
"What makes you different?"

Sunday, September 15, 2013

365QOD- Day953

Communicate

"9. Deal And Communicate With People Effectively: No person is an island. Learn to understand and motivate others."-IBD ninth of ten secrets to success

Communication with others and self is very important. What and how we say things to others and ourselves could build us or destroy us.

Long time ago I read a John Maxwell book on **21 Irrefutable Laws of Leadership**. In it he graphically explained the results of being able to move people towards a common goal. He showed a graph on which he showed a line to the right to indicate a person's effectiveness. This was a rather one dimensional. You can work on yourself and the best you could get to is a 10 on a ten scale. But if you improve your communication then the graph adds a second vertical axis.

Now suppose that your effectiveness is 7 and your team is a 8. Your total effectiveness is 56. By improving yourself to an 8 only moves it to 64 but if your team becomes a 10 then you guys become an 80. A drastic improvement for the whole team.

Today's question is:
" How effective are you at communicating with others and yourself?"

Monday, September 16, 2013

365QOD- Day954

Honest

"**10. Be Honest And Dependable**; Take Responsibly: Otherwise, numbers 1-9 won't matter."-IBD tenth of ten secrets to success

I also believe that without honesty the other nine traits are meaningless. Interesting thing about honesty is that you cannot fake it.

As a leader you can delay giving information to your team but once you lie one time, you will never be trusted ever again. Your team will remember the lie(s) and hesitantly follow you. This delay is hurtful in making forward progress and it could lead to eventual failure.

One thing I always say is that it is easier to remember one truth than ten lies. It never stops at one lie. That first lie had to be covered by another and another until you have to think about what you originally said. This is such an energy waster.

Today's question is:
"How do you keep yourself honest?"

Friday, October 11, 2013

365QOD- Day979

Risk Profile

"I get a knot in my stomach"-Anonymous

In an article by Jocelyn Glei I learned of five primary types of risks. I would like to explore these in next five posts.

First type of risk is **Physical**.

I am sure you have heard the quoted expression. Physically you feel that what you are about to do will put your body in danger. You might not get the knot but your hands might get sweaty. Your ears might get red. The response is very unique to you as a person.

I mentioned in another post that I do not like to handle snakes. So I do not. The risk is a physical fear. What if I get bitten? The reality is that if I handled a snake that the probability of getting bitten is so small. So my conclusion is to get over this fear next time I am around a snake. This is my way of using logic to convince myself that the physical risk is not worth fearing.

How about bungee jumping? I also don't care for extreme heights. So jumping over is a physical risk that the rubber band would break. In reality it is not the fear of heights but fear of jumping into the unknown.

I better start with the snakes.

Today's question is:
"What do you consider a physical risk?"

Monday, October 14, 2013

365QOD- Day982

Financial Risk

"Money, I got to have it..."-song lyric

I think of each dollar as 100 soldiers. Ever one of these soldiers deserves our attention and respect. Without the attention and respect we are exposing ourselves to greater financial risk.

Most of us will easily earn more than a million dollars in our life. But most of us will never become millionaires. Why? It is our exposure to risk.

I believe that our mindsets are not set up to become millionaires. We tend to expose ourselves daily to poor financial decisions. Decisions that just take money out of our pocket. $5 Latte anyone?

We are letting our soldiers go into fights and letting them get killed. Even better, we give then away to others by making questionable purchases that have use in only the short term. This does not allow us to grow our army. We put ourselves in a position where we are constantly trading our time soldiers, seconds, for money soldiers, pennies. In other words, we work to spend.

Today's question is:
"Are you giving away your soldiers?"

Tuesday, October 15, 2013

365QOD- Day983

Intellectual Risk

"I am smarter than that."- Self encouragement

I believe that our intelligence can grow over time. How? If we choose to expose ourselves to continuous learning then our whole life will make us smarter.

As you might have noticed, our world is moving at an incredible pace. If you are not drowning in email then you have not checked it yet. There are so many channels on TV that you can easily just keep flipping without stopping to see a whole show. How about the number of new books that are published each day?

The world around us provides us with a ton of new data. It is so much data that we seldom have time to convert it into information. But we must with some work. That data can then become knowledge and over time lead to wisdom.

It all starts with exposing ourselves to new information. Notice that I said information and not data. Information is processed data. It is one step above.

This is where intellectual risk comes into play. What if we are not smart enough to absorb the information? Or even better, not smart enough to find the information we need?

Today's question is:
"Are you exposing yourself to continuous learning?"

Saturday, October 12, 2013

365QOD- Day980

Social Risk

"To be social or not be social, that is the question now."- RT

Do you remember starting a new job? You were the new kid on the block. The one everyone is curious about.

In that one and many other social situations people want to get to know you better. So how much of you do you reveal? You want to be social but you also want to be guarded is my advice. There should be a bit of mystery to you and your life.

I believe that the more people know about us the more social risk we expose ourselves. With this, I am not saying not to share a portion of your life but sharing everything exposes your many weaknesses.

So what is the right amount? I believe that 20% of your life is a good guideline. It is the 80/20 rule. This leaves a lot of mystery for people to want to find out over time.

The number will grow over time towards 80 but it should not ever get to 100. I believe that this also holds true in relationships as well as marriage. It keeps the relationship fresh.

Today's question is:
"How much of yourself do you reveal?"

Sunday, October 13, 2013

365QOD- Day981

Emotional Risk

"This is going to make me cry"-men's ultimate weakness

Many years ago I sat on a beach and read **The Power of Full Engagement**. I doubt that a week has passed since that I have not referenced it in conversations. The book teaches us about four energies we all share: physical, mental, emotional, and spiritual.

I believe that most of us guys tend to ignore the emotional dimension to our lives. This choice exposes us to a lot of emotional risk. How?

Suppose your spouse needs one hour per day of your undivided attention. This might not be a solid hour but split over many smaller chunks of time. That is what she expects, but suppose you only give her 30 minutes for an extended amount of time. Eventually this creates tension and you will have to spend hours trying to get back on track. These hours are usually spent arguing.

It is the classic pay me now or pay me later. If you were to average out the time spend connecting with arguing and the approach that uses daily emotional connection, I bet it will average out to the one hour need.

The difference is in spreading out your emotional risk vs. concentrating it during arguments. Which one is better? I believe that setting time aside every day is a better choice. That way you exercise your emotional muscles every day and they get stronger.

Today's question is:
"What emotional risk did you expose yourself to today?"

Monday, February 11, 2013

365QOD- Day737

"Q: From the entrepreneurs you've worked with, what has collectively been the biggest barrier to their success? How do you suggest people overcome this?

A: More than anything, the key is staying focused. I tell a lot of my clients to look at their life like an iPad and to identify what "apps" they have open.

Most people have way too many apps, or projects open. What happens when a computer has too many apps open? One, the processor speed slows down. And two, worst case scenario, a crash can occur."- Entrepreneur Coach Antonio Neves on Finding Focus and the Power of Storytelling

I also believe that most people have way too many apps or projects open. I am definitely one of them. Even though I currently only have one job, I have many projects.

The rest of the quote is spot on also. Since my attention is divided then my brain feels like it has slowed down. Even better, at the end of the year I feel burned out and need to recharge by sitting on the beach for a week or two.

So what? Well, I think the secret is to focus on one project and place a hold on the other ones until the chosen one is done. This is easier said than done. I often start with great energy but then something else looks shinier and more interesting. I move onto that and then after some time come back to the first project. Eventually both get done but it is definitely not a sequential process of one thing gets done and I move onto the next one.

I have learned to accept that fault in me as long as I am executing something. BUT what I see as a weakness is the idea of 'too many apps open'. Maybe I need to limit myself to 2-3 projects in front of me. Maybe it should be only two? Which one is priority?

Today's question is:
"How many apps do you have open at this time?"

Sunday, April 21, 2013

365QOD- Day806

"So the Muse (daughter of Zeus and Mnemosyne) whispered in Beethoven's ear. Maybe she hummed a few dah-dah-dah-DUM bars into a million other ears. But no one else heard her. Only Beethoven got it." - My paraphrase of War of Art by Steven Pressfield

Many of times I have said that when God gives us an idea he takes out an insurance against us by giving it to many others. God does not care who executes the idea but that the idea gets executed.

The quote above is another way of saying the same. I love his version.

I spent the day reading this book and thinking about the concept of Resistance. Maybe we do not hear the sounds because we are resisting. We have to be open to hearing God's voice and see his fingerprints in our lives?

The resistance leads us to live two lives. As Steven says, **"The life that we live, and the unlived life within us. Between the two stands Resistance"**

Today's question is:
" Are you hearing the dah-dah-dah-DUM bars or are you Resisting?"

Friday, May 3, 2013

365QOD- Day819

"Good conversation is as stimulating as black coffee, and just as hard to sleep after."- Anne Murrow Lindbergh

Last night I had a conversation with a new friend. We talked about ideas.

He started telling me what he is working on. I told him what challenges are stretching me.

In the end I felt refreshed. My mind stretched. But like the quote, it was hard to sleep and not think about the ideas we discussed.

Today's question is:
" **Do you feel energized after a great conversation?**"

Saturday, May 11, 2013

365QOD- Day827

"... you got to become one with the bicycle"- Tommy Hendricks

Last night I was talking with Tommy. We started talking about the keys to success.

Tommy gave a great example. In his example he asked the question if anyone ever learned how to ride a bicycle without falling? The obvious answer is that no one ever learned to ride a bicycle without falling.

The effort to ride the bicycle involves falling a few times until you understand the balance required to not fall. But once you master the balance, you become one with the bicycle.

This idea holds true for bicycle riding, book writing, cookie making, business building, etc. you become one with" it", whatever it means to you.

Today's question is:
" What are you one with?"

Sunday, May 19, 2013

365QOD- Day835

"I am up for the challenge" - my response

A couple of days ago I finished listening to a six CD set by Jim Rohn on changing one's life. There were many great ideas in it. In this and tomorrow posts I like to discuss a couple of life challenges.

According to Jim, life poses two challenges that we should pursue. The first challenge is:

How do we develop ourselves to our maximum potential?

I love this question. Often we are afraid to go after what we want because our best might not be good enough. So we pull back from giving it our all. In order to give it our all we must develop our full potential. This takes wisdom to self-evaluate where your gaps are and to figure out how to fill them.

Today's question is:
" What do you need to do to develop to your full potential?"

Monday, May 20, 2013
365QOD- Day836

"That is easy."- answer to the first challenge

Jim Rohn's second challenge that he believed life poses is:

How do we wisely use all of our resources?

Resources that we have are money, time, attention, love, etc. If for a moment we just focus on time we quickly notice that we are very often not the guardians of our time. Someone walks into your office and you drop everything to accommodate them.

Similarly, we trend to watch the Pennies while dollars get blown away. That pop in the machine is a dollar but that dollar adds up over time to a fortune.

Same thing with the other resources. We tend to waste them until we feel the lack of not having them.

Today's a question is:
" **How do you make sure you wisely use your resources?**"

Tuesday, May 21, 2013

365QOD- Day837

"Fundamental Attribution Error- the tendency to ignore context and attribute an individual's success or failure solely to inherent qualities" - definition

When I read this line it made me think about fixed vs. flexible mindset. The fixed mindset believes that all results are due to being smart. The flexible mindset believes in working hard and figuring things out as you move through the challenge. To me, inherent qualities bring up fixed, born with ideas.

After reading the definition a second time, I noticed the 'ignore context' portion. A success in one field does not translate into success in another field. If that was true then Michael Jordan would be also the greatest baseball player and the greatest NBA executive. He was average in baseball and in being a boss.

Success in one arena could be due to your skill set, your willingness to fight for what you want, your focus, etc. The place where you fight is also critical. A great boxer in a rink might not do so good in a bar fight.

Today's question is:
" Do you consider the context along with your skill set?"

Wednesday, June 19, 2013

365QOD- Day866

"How we hold our bodies affects our minds, confidence, and our performance. For instance, if you stand up straight and walk with purposeful long strides, it will make you feel more assured and powerful"- A.J. Jacobs

Amen! I believe this to be very true. No doubt whatsoever. But there is a problem.

I do not always follow this advice. I slouch. My back is getting strained unnecessarily. In the past I have had neck pain so bad that I had to take pain killers and do physical therapy.

So if I know this, why is it that I do not just do what I know? The gap is somewhere in my mind. My brain knows that poor posture leads to problems. The back and neck know how it feels when I do not walk purposely. The only thing left is the mind.

The mind must be controlling the brain and body for whatever reason. I have to retrain my mind by walking purposely. In my opinion I have to catch myself and correct myself continuously until I close the gap.

Today's question is:
"How would you retrain your mind to eliminate a gap?"

Sunday, June 23, 2013

365QOD- Day 870

"Innovation is driven by questions that are original, bold, counterintuitive, and perceptive... Coming up with the right question, the one that casts a familiar challenge in a new light, is an art and science in itself. It demands that the questioner be able to look at existing reality from multiple viewpoints, including, perhaps most importantly, that of the' naive outsider'"- Warren Burger author of Glimmer

As you know, this blog is all about reading, pausing to think, and asking questions. This quote is very informative on how to ask the right question.

To break it apart: it has to
1 to be original, bold, counterintuitive, and perceptive
2 to cast a new light on a familiar challenge
3 to question existing reality
4 consider multiple viewpoints
5 bring the freshness of an naive outsider

Do you need all of these? Probably not all but most would make it great. I can see needing to meet at least three out of five criteria.

Today's question is:
"How do you know you are asking the innovative questions?"

Wednesday, June 26, 2013

365QOD- Day873

"To achievers are improvisers not perfectionists. If you want to create more success in your life you have to move forward not knowing all the answers "- Douglas Vermeeren

We all love certainty. When we come up with an idea then our baby must be perfect. This in the end leads to frustration and eventual stopping of any forward momentum.

The wisdom in this quote is to realize that success is most often a road with many places where you will have to improvise. Knowing this means that you have to be comfortable being uncomfortable. It is like moving into the dark without any light in front of you.

So forget about certainty and keep moving forward into the uncomfortable. Stop seeking perfection and enjoy the forward motion.

Today's question is:
"Can you move forward into uncertainty?"

Monday, July 1, 2013

365QOD- Day878

"Courage is resistance to fear, mastery of fear- not absence of fear"- Mark Twain

I think that delaying is misunderstood. Most people believe that delay is most often due because a person is considering many options. I do not.

To me, delaying is fear. If you make a decision you have to trust yourself to be able to adapt your strategy if your choice is not working out the way you think it should. You believe more in yourself than the fear. To me that is the definition of courage.

However, as the quote advises, you might still have fear but you are mastering it by believing in your ability to overcome the obstacles. You believe that you are bigger than your obstacles.

Today's question is:
"How do you make yourself believe in yourself?"

Sunday, July 21, 2013

365QOD- Day897

"Two out of three?" -a request made after a loss

I started reading a new book called **Big Dog** by Po Bronson and Ashley Merryman. The book discusses the science of winning and losing. In the book there are couple of case studies that highlight reactions.

The first study forced novices to in one day learn how to skydive and to make three jumps. The study collected saliva stress data before and after each jump. Interestingly, the stress level after each jump reduced by 25%. By the third jump the stress level reduced to a level we experience if we are late and stuck in traffic.

In a second study seasoned dancers were monitored using the same type of saliva samples during a ballroom competition. Some of the dancers had been practicing and competing for more than a decade. Their bodies have in a sense memorized the movements. The interesting find was that their levels did not go down like the skydiving case.

So what was the difference? The difference was that the ballroom dancers were in a competition against others and the skydivers were simply focused on what they needed to do.

Competition is great for forcing us to raise our level but as the study shows creates a great amount of stress even in seasoned competitors. The key is to learn how to completely relax during competition. The authors of The Power of Full Engagement book claimed that how quickly tennis players relaxed between points made the difference between being a winner or a good player.

Today's question is:
"How do you respond to competition?"

Thursday, August 15, 2013

365QOD- Day922

Say That Again!

"..Knowledge.."- Richard Perrin

I sat through an exam prep course this week that Richard instructed. During the presentation he said something that caught my attention. It was similar to something I say all of the time.

In the past I wrote how we are drowning in data. Sometimes we take that data and convert it into information. Lastly, rarely do we take that information and reach wisdom. Pretty cool.

Well Richard said pretty much the same thing but after information inserted knowledge before reaching wisdom. Immediately my mind started evaluating if this is a needed addition to the model.

So data is raw. Information is processed data. For example I get raw data and when I graph it I notice that the data is linear. That is information. Now taking that information I use math to determine a unique equation that fits that data. The line is of the form $y = mx + b$ where I get unique values for m (slope) and x (y-intercept). Lastly, I get to wisdom by realizing that the two variables that are graphed are success and reading. Since the line goes up it indicates that the more you read different sources the more successful you are. So I decide that I should expand my reading selection.

In the end I see why Richard added knowledge as a step on the way to wisdom.

Today's question is:
"Do you see the stepping stones from data to information to knowledge to wisdom for your problem?"

Thursday, August 22, 2013

365QOD- Day929

Stop in the Middle

"When you hit your daily word goal, stop. Stop even if you're in the middle of a sentence. Especially if you're in the middle of a sentence. That way , when you sit down at the keyboard the next day, your five or ten words are already ordained, so that you get a little push before you begin your work...."- Cory Doctorow

I printed out a bunch of articles to read this weekend and this one quite was on top. I read it and immediately could see a couple examples where this works and does not work for me. Let me share them with you.

Several years ago I worked in a refinery and had a large L shape desk. At the beginning of the day I would start working and by the end of the day you could barely see my desk from the papers and prints. Before I left for the day I used to pick up all of my papers, put them in folders, and get them off my desk. Next day the cycle stated all over again. My productivity was very high.

This is an example where I left nothing undone and it worked for me. I was very productive. Interestingly, I never clear my desk any more on my new job. Because I do not, I do believe that I am less productive as a result of this.

The second example I would like to share deals with writing blog posts. Often times I see something I like and enter the idea in a new post. I might even write a sentence or two. This serves to get me going when I have time to finish writing the post. This is an example of stopping in the middle. I just start without spending time planning my actions.

What I see, at least for me, is that the idea of stopping in the middle is good for creative work but not for repetitive tasks. The clean slate allows me to take a few minutes to come up with the best plan before I execute. The stop in the middle strategy helps me to continue the plan execution.

Today's question:
"Do you ever use the little push of the stop in the middle strategy?"

Friday, August 23, 2013
365QOD- Day930

This for That

"The meeting requests that note jump to the top of my list are the few, very smart entrepreneur who say, 'I'd like to have coffee to bounce an idea off of you and in exchange I'll tell you all about what we learned about cc'."- Steve Blank's advice for those seeking his or other busy folks' time

Often times we want something that somebody has. The most priceless thing we can ask from another is to give us some of their time. This might even be the reason why we tend to do things when people are talking with us.

Steve offers a suggestion of trading something for that time. In his suggestion he offers a learning that the person might be interested in. Brilliant!

I think that this would work if the person is interested in the new information. If you know the person of whom you are asking for time then you should be able to guess what is of interest to them. Another thing that this strategy accomplishes is to place you on par with the person. You are equal if you are trading.

Today's question is:
"Do you trade information?"

Thursday, October 3, 2013

365QOD- Day971

Of Service

"We know we need to listen, but that is not enough. More impotently we need to execute and give our customers what they have been asking for- and fast"- Alison Johnson Marketing VP at Apple

When I was young I remember my mom telling me that when someone asks me to do something that they mean right now. According to my mom, doing what they ask you to do tomorrow has less of an impact.

As adults we tend to delay our execution. Alison reminds us that we need to give the customer what they want and it must be done quickly. So if we fail to execute then we definitely fail at fast execution.

I believe that we live in an ADD world. We are all running around trying to do too much at once. We do not know how to say no. This is why we over commit and under perform. By saying no we could reduce the over-commit portion and improve our performance.

We need a pull system instead of a push system. In this system we pull a job when we are done with one. Not just simply adding jobs without finishing one.

Today's question is:
"Have you ever used a pull system?"

Thursday, October 10, 2013

365QOD- Day978

Write Badly

"Have the Courage to Write Badly"- title by Herbert Lui

I have to admit that I write badly most of the time. This should not be a surprise to you. Since I write with passion I tend to write quickly in order to capture my thoughts and my blogger will substitute words on my cell phone Swype keyboard that I did not intend.

This is an excuse. When I do take the time to read the posts after creating them I will often find several mistakes easily. So I can edit my work but due to my rushing I choose not to. At the end of the year I take the time to rewrite the stories before they make it in my books. My books are, in my opinion, well written because I have debugged them.

So I find the time to do it properly the second or third time but not the first time. This is nuts and a waste of time. So since this is silly I have decided to drop rewriting the story and instead focusing on reading the poorly written pieces out loud before I hit publish.

Today's question us:
"Do you have the courage to write badly?"

Friday, October 18, 2013

365QOD- Day986

Success Vs. Confidence

"Competence leads to confidence, but not vice versa."-Thomas Chamorro Premusic article
Confidence Does not Lead to Success

One of the self-help bits of advice that you get is to "fake it until you make it". If you don't know what to do then simply ask yourself, "What would I do if I knew what to do?" But this article completely disproves this idea.

According to the article there is only a 30% correlation between success and career confidence. In other words we would only be 20% more accurate than if we just guessed (50/50). So what does this mean?

Most of us would say that confident people are more successful. But that does not hold as a truth. According to the article, being talented makes you more competent which in turn leads to make you more confident and successful.
In other words,
                Talent =>competence= >confidence =>success   (TCCS)

The path is one directional. You can't fake the success hoping to build your confidence which will lead to competence and ultimately result in a talent. It does not work in that direction.

So how important is talent? I do believe that we often find some things are easier for us and they appear as talent. In my life I have taken things that were NOT talents and worked on them until they become easier. In other words I became competent. To get to confidence I needed to be passionate about improving and continuing to learn and improve. Doing all this lead to success. Maybe not as big success as if I started with a natural talent.

Today's question is:
"What is an example of TCCS in your life?"

Wednesday, October 30, 2013

365QOD- Day998

The Start and the End

"Start strong"- My thought

I started doing something this weekend that I have not done in years. Many years ago I created a time and energy management system that is great. I followed it for years so I know it works. But then I stopped.

This weekend I sat down on Sunday night and planned out my whole week. I placed all of the big pieces that would make the week a success. The big pieces are the most important parts of my week.

This event made me notice an article on what some CEOs do after work. They try to cram in a little family time and then go back to working.

Wow! What a lack of balance. Is doing emails till 12 the best way to recharge for the next day? I doubt it.

I believe that you should do weekly planning on Sundays, review the plan for the day at the start, and conduct a detailed review at the end of the day. But once you get home, be present for your family.

Today's question is:
"How do you start and end your days?"

Friday, November 15, 2013

365QOD- Day1014

Parkinson's Pareto

"Combining two ideas makes it orders of magnitude more powerful"- My thought

Recently I read an interview of Time Ferriss by Derek Sivers that was done back in 2008. The post I wrote about Parkinson's Law was inspired by that interview. Today's post is no different.

In many past posts I have talked about the 80/20 principle that Vilfredo Pareto originated. 20% of my activities contribute to 80% of my success. The vital few are hard to identify while moving through the noise.

Tim Ferriss offers advice on how to combine these two ideas, **"With the 80/20 principle, you're limiting your tasks to the critical few versus the trivial many to decrease the amount of time required. Then with Parkinson's Law, you're constraining the time allocated to force yourself to focus on the critical few"**

Brilliant strategy! Limit yourself to the vital 20% of the tasks and give yourself a time limit to get them done. Simple idea on paper but I think that the challenge is the getting clear as to what is the 20% and what is not critically important. But once you are clear then the combination become like adding 1+1 and getting 3 as the result.

Today's question is:

"Can you limit yourself to the vital 20% of your tasks and give yourself a time limit?"

Wednesday, December 4, 2013

365QOD- Day1033

Busyness

"Being busy is a form of laziness-lazy thinking and indiscriminate action"- Tim Ferris

The other day I just had two appointments. One at 8-8:30 and the other one from 3-4 in the afternoon. The rest of the day was left unscheduled.

In the resent few weeks I have been getting better at using my time energy management system and getting more things done. This requires me to plan weekly and check in daily. For some reason this day was left unplanned.

So what happened? As the quote teaches, I was very busy. But my busyness was focused on indiscriminate actions. All of them needed to be done but maybe most of them could have been done another day. This was without thought and fits Tim's first prediction-lazy thinking. According to Tim, **"Being busy is most often used as a guise for avoiding the few critically important but uncomfortable actions."**

Maybe that is why I felt very unproductive and down at the end of the day. I fought a war in which I won all of the small battles but yet lost the war.

Today's question is:
"Do you catch yourself when your day is full of indiscriminate actions?"

Saturday, December 7, 2013

365QOD- Day1036

Winning Contests

"Winning races is nice, but it was never transformative. The pleasure doesn't come from running the fastest you've run, it comes from just the experience of very moderately testing yourself. I find that kind of nice"- Malcolm Gladwell

This weekend during a visit to my favorite bookstore in Houston I read an article on Malcolm. Since I was reading his new book it made sense to get to know a more personal side of this brilliant thinker. I learned things that surprised me.

One of the things that surprised me was how great of a runner he was when he was young. He even won races and championships in Canada. Pretty impressive for someone that looks like he would be afraid to step onto a track.

The quote teaches us why he excelled in this sport. It seems that Malcolm realized that incremental improvements and tests are necessary to transform one's performance. He had used the process to become the best he could be as a racer.

What is interesting is that once he realized that he could no longer be the best he moved on. He knew that his body could not take the punishment and that he had no Olympic hopes. To me that is wisdom in knowing when you have reached the peak of your potential and need to move on to something else.

Today's question is:
"Do you know when you have reached the peak of your potential and need to move on?"

Tuesday, January 28, 2014

365QOD- Day1088

Two Mistakes Per Year

"People who don't take risks generally make about two big mistakes per year. People who do take risks generally make about two big mistakes per year."- Peter F. Drucker

I happen to work in the chemical industry that is very risk averse. The potential for loss of life is too great to be accepting of more risk. So anything we do must go through rigorous process by which the risk level is quantified, understood, mitigated, and eventually accepted.

But most of our lives are made up of things that will not result in a loss of life. So to be afraid of making mistakes is silly. I believe that for most adverse things that could occur to me that I could recover to the same state or better in a short time. Without having this belief, I would be paralyzed.

The interesting advice that Drucker offers is that no matter what our approach is that we will make two big mistakes. Acceptance of that wisdom should lead us to be free to risk a bit more. Hopefully, our lives end up being more rewarding once the risk has been accepted and conquered.

Today's question is:

"What two big mistakes did you make last year?"

Teamwork

Saturday, February 9, 2013

365QOD- Day735

"If I hire someone just like me then I have doubled the company's strengths and doubled its weaknesses" – my response

I spoke these words recently during an interview. I was asked, "What do you look for in candidates?" I strongly feel that we must hire people that are different than ourselves.

In my opinion, most interviewers are asking themselves a simple question, "Is this person just like me?" The closer you are to their vision of themselves then the more likely you are to get the job.

It requires a lot of self-awareness to be able to be honest and realize that we all bring strengths and weaknesses to a job. In order for a team to be stronger we need to hire people that complete the team not just duplicate team members.

Unfortunately, most folks are stuck on this replica idea. Their belief is that if the person is just like them they will succeed just like them. And after all they are doing the interview so it must be true.

Today's question is:
"How do you handle working with very different people?"

Friday, December 6, 2013

365QOD- Day1035

Quality of Your Colleagues

"The reason academics are so obsessed with who their colleagues are is not just prestige: it is productivity. The person that we hire and sits in the office next door influences our creativity and our thinking. This extends to private sector research"- Enrico Moretti

The other day I had a conversation with a guy from New Jersey. He has moved down to Texas for the opportunity. BUT during the conversation it became obvious that he misses his previous life.

According to him, he lived in a place where most of big cities on the east coast were within one-two hour striking distance. With this closeness he could take advantage of the different cultures and groups in all of these cities.

I immediately recalled this quote. He was talking about closeness to centers as the driver in his quality of life. The quote teaches us that closeness to productive and creative colleagues improves our own productivity and quality of work.

Unfortunately, it is very difficult to peak into a team before joining it in the private sector. We might be able to look at the leader of the team by looking at their LinkedIn profile. Access to other colleagues is close to impossible. Maybe that should be a standard question during interviews?

Today's question is:
"Are you satisfied with the quality of your colleagues?"

Tuesday, December 24, 2013

365QOD- Day1053

Purpose Driven Team- Part 1

"What are we doing?" Lee Colan's first question in Inc. magazine article

Leaders often get a vision. It is clear to us where we want the team to go. Unfortunately, it is often clear as mud to our followers.

This question is the first of four questions that we will ask ourselves. This question forces us to identify the team goals. In my opinion, vision without goals is simply a thought in the leader's head.

This is where setting smart goals has its purpose. Make sure your goals are:

Specific

Measurable

Achievable

Relevant

Time bound

So in order to help your team become more purpose driven help them go through a goal exercise that translates your vision into specific smart goals.

Today's question is:

"What smart goals is your team working towards achieving?"

Wednesday, December 25, 2013

365QOD- Day1054

Purpose Driven Team- Part 2

"What are we doing to get there?" Lee Colan's second question in Inc. article

In first part of the purpose driven team we looked at translating a leader's vision into concrete smart goals. I simply applied the smart acronym in order to quantify them. But having the goals is not enough.

The smart goals need to be translated into concrete execution plans. In my understanding I see the translation from vision to goals as figuring out the "what". Next we need to translate the what into "how" territory by creating plans.

When creating plans we need to consider the

Scope,

Schedule,

Costs

These are the traditional triple constraints But I believe that **Risk** also needs to be considered. The team should consider what risks can occur and get in the way of reaching the goals. Many projects fail because of lack of risk awareness and plans to handle them.

Today's question is:

"How do you convert your smart goals into specific plans?"

Thursday, December 26, 2013

365QOD- Day1055

Purpose Driven Team- Part 3

"How can I contribute?" Lee Colan's third question in Inc. magazine

The first piece to developing purpose driven team are to transfer the vision into smart goals. Second piece is to create specific plans to drive towards those goals. So what could be missing by just doing these two steps?

The first two steps are group driven. Now we need to assign personal roles that each team member will accomplish. In other words we need to transition the we goals into a me goal.

Each team member has to feel that their role will contribute towards the goals. It usually works best if each member chooses role which they feel they can best contribute in. Don't assume that team member who was a star at doing one thing will be great at doing everything. This halo affect can demoralize a key member. By allowing the team to choose their role instead of assigning them gets them to buy into the goal as being their own.

Today's question is:

"Do you allow your team to choose their role in goal achieving?"

Friday, December 27, 2013

365QOD- Day1056

Purpose Driven Team- Part 4

"What's in it for me?" Lee Colan's forth question

Most corporate incentive systems are either carrot or stick type. Either you punish the employee for not achieving or reward them for succeeding. Let us focus on the reward aspect.

I have seen people get rewarded and they are angry with the boss or company. Everyone does not value money as the only reward. Rewards are only meaningful if the individual values it. If I value time but my boss rewards me by giving me financial bonus I would only see it as a partial fulfillment. I would prefer maybe a smaller reward with time off to enjoy it.

I believe that a new reward type that we will see is to provide employees with an experience. Maybe a paid trip to a dental mission in Africa would be the most fulfilling experience that an employee would find most rewarding? Maybe the ability to work in a soup kitchen every Friday? Reward is very individual and needs to be understood.

Today's question is:

"What reward do you value the most?"

Transitions

Sunday, December 29, 2013

365QOD- Day1058

Becoming Real

"You become. It takes a long time. That's why it doesn't happen often to people who break easily, or have sharp edges, or have to be carefully kept. Generally, by the time you are Real, most of your hair has been loved off, and your eyes drop out, and you get loose in the joint and very shabby. But these things don't matter at all, because once you are Real you can't be ugly except to people who don't understand." - The velveteen rabbit

This quote was on a painting that I saw in a gallery the other day. How could I walk away without writing it down? I could not.

I believe that I have many sharp edges inside me. At times those edges get in my way of becoming Real. Even with this, I at least realize the need to become Real.

As the quote teaches, the process takes a long time. It requires us to become. To me this means taking the time daily to reflect on one's life and how to transition to a better level. Level of what? It could be a level of anything. As I wrote in Day1057, it could be reaching a new level of happiness. For some of us it could be reaching a level of thinking, financial, love, flow, focus, etc.

Identifying the change in level, while smoothing the edges, is the key. But retaining the level is critical. If you slide back after becoming something you are not any better off than your old self. You know what it took to get there but not how to stay there. Note that the gains do not have to be great but they have to be continuously gotten and kept.

Today's question is:
"Are you becoming Real?"

Zen

Tuesday, March 19, 2013

365QOD- Day773

"Bamboo is flexible, bending with the wind but never breaking, capable of adapting to any circumstance. It suggests resistance, meaning that we have the ability to bounce back even from the most difficult time...Your ability to thrive depends, in the end, on your attitude to your life circumstances. Take everything in stride with grace, putting forth energy when it is needed, yet always staying calm inwardly"- Ping Fu, Bend Not Break book

Recently I have been getting up at five and doing yoga for a half hour. Initially, it was somewhat of a chore to get up and stretch but now if I do not do it I feel the difference. I am more relaxed when I do.

Most animals stretch when they wake up. There is a reason why many of the stretches are named after animals: downward dog, cat, cow, frog, cobra, etc. Maybe there is wisdom to stretching first thing in the morning?

I have also noticed that I not only feel good that I have stretched but also my mind is calmer due to the breathing portion of yoga. The calm typically lasts for a few hours. By noon I note no difference. Maybe I need to do a lunch session to get it back?

Today's question is:
"How do you begin your day?"

Saturday, May 4, 2013

365QOD- Day820

"How would you live your life if you only had six months to live?" - A big question

It seems at times we lack clarity. We feel that we do not get it done today, we can always get to it tomorrow. Whatever the 'it' we are working or thinking about now.

While listening to an audio CD by Joe Polish with Brian Tracy, Brian asked this question. He said that he felt most of us would be forced to focus if that was the reality for us.

For most of us that life or death situation does not seem real. So we delay. And delay because we feel that tomorrow will always come.

The most extreme position is to imagine if this is your last day. This is a Zen idea.

Today's question is:
" If today was your last day, how would you spend it? With who? Doing what? Eating what? Saying good bye to who? Finishing what?"

Sunday, May 5, 2013

365QOD- Day821

"Wherever you are is the entry point" - Rumi

Most of us expect a magic starting point with trumpets announcing the beginning of something big. Reality never lives up to this fantasy.

Everything has a beginning and an end. Both the beginning and the end are often very fuzzy. You seem never certain that you are just starting or that you are completely done.

So with this in mind, Rumi's advice is a jewel. It doesn't matter if the start gun had gone off, just begin. It doesn't matter if the finish tape had been removed, just keep going.

Both the beginning and the end are entry points. Just continue.

Today's question is:
"What is this adventure an entry point for?"

Monday, June 24, 2013

365QOD- Day871

"Only put off until tomorrow what you are willing to die having left undone"- Pablo Picasso

I read this quote the other day in a group of 50 success quotes. Ever since I read it, I could not get it out of my mind. Here are some of my thoughts about it.

I believe that we tend to spend most of our lives in two time modes:
    yesterday-now
and
    now-tomorrow.

The only thing that those two modes have in common is the now. Unfortunately, we tend to forget this.

Our lives are either spent reliving the past or planning for the future. But the magic only occurs in the now. This why it is a 'present'.

As the quote instructs we should not waste our time putting off our dreams till tomorrow because it might never come. If it is that important to you then continue working on it today until you are spent. For if you are to die tonight, you would have done all you could towards completing it.

Today's question is:
"What dream are you willing to leave undone forever?"

Tuesday, June 25, 2013

365QOD- Day872

"Tell me, **what is it your plan to do with your one wild and precious life**"- **poet Mary Oliver**

How many of us would classify our lives as wild? Probably even less of us are aware how precious life is truly.

For me the second part is easy. I believe it deeply. I realize that each day is a gift that I was given that at the end of the day gets thrown away. I have 20000 presents left to enjoy.

The first part of the quote caused me to pause. My life is anything but wild. I live a pretty simple life. Most people would even classify it as somewhat boring.

Maybe I am missing many things by the way I live? Maybe I need to introduce a bit of the wild in my day to day to feel the effect of it.

Today's question is:
"Do you see your life as wild and precious?"

Friday, July 5, 2013

365QOD- Day882

" Hapifork, an electronic fork that vibrates and lights up when you're eating too fast connects via USB to your computer our via wireless to your smart phone to track your eating habits"- Entrepreneur magazine 6/13

I have a problem when I eat. The speed with which I consume my meals is too fast. Often times my stomach has no chance to recognize that I am full until it is too late.

This invention is brilliant. It brings you into the now so that you can note your eating speed and provides a record of it. You can then study yourself and learn how to eat better. What the idea also made me think was how we are starting to use more tools to help us to do better.

Why is it that I need a vibrating fork? Because I am not aware at those moments. That should be my focus. The tool could over time make me realize that I am eating too fast and too much but it cannot make me aware. In a sense over time I should use the fork reminders less and less.

Today's question is:
"What tool could you use to make you more aware of your habits? "

Monday, October 7, 2013

365QOD- Day975

The Man with Two Watches

"So why do you wear two watches all of the time?"-my question to a friend

Many years ago I worked with a friend of mine whose name is Ivy. He is a very interesting person with whom I have had many conversations over the years.

The quote above was the start of one such conversation. I was curious as to why he always wore two watches, one on each hand, at all times. So I asked the question.

Ivy told me that he has a young wife and that he also has two watches. Every day he makes a choice to wear both watches in order for them to be worn. He said that every night he also makes love with his wife as if it was his last time.

I could not resist asking why? His answer was that he did not want to die and for some guy to come in and find brand new watches and a wife that had not been loved. So he lived his every day trying to use to the fullest what made up his world in order for their value to be zero to anyone else.

Today's question is:
"Do you appreciate and use everything in your world?"

Saturday, February 1, 2014

365QOD- Day1091

Beginner's Mind

"Why would you go to a school and start as a white belt?"- My question to a friend

Many years ago while I was working in a steel mill, there was one guy who was unusual. He would spend his lunch hour working out. So I joined him.

He was in his middle forties and told me that he has serious arthritis. In order to reduce the effects he worked out every day doing martial arts. He had done this for 20+ years. You would never guess that he had arthritis.

So we would work out by doing different martial art forms. He was a great teacher and a very different thinker. I enjoyed learning from him.

One day he told me a story how he had recently signed up as a white belt in a new martial arts school. I thought this was weird. He was a high ranking black belt in multiple styles. It just did not make sense for him to go backwards and start as a white belt. Apparently, this was something that he had done many times.

I kept thinking and thinking as to why someone with great knowledge would go back and start at the very bottom. His answer to me was that he knows the basics very well BUT maybe the person teaching him learned them differently. The funny thing was that many of his teachers were lower ranking than him.

This is when I learned that we sometimes need to humble ourselves and consider even less knowledgeable people around us as teachers. I understood that a beginner's mind brings freshness to something that you might have done a million times. It is very hard to be that humble BUT it is worth the effort.

I adapted his belief many years later when I taught martial arts as a white belt for years. The looks on the parent's faces as I was teaching their black belt students told me that I was doing the right thing. I was teaching them all to be open to learning and that a black belt was just a learning point not an end to a journey.

Today's question is:

"Do you have a beginner's mind?"

Conclusion

When someone learns that I have been writing a blog for three years, the first question is, "So what have you learned?" I immediately smile. They are looking for a result.

To me the three years have been a journey. I am addicted to writing the posts and when I do not write I feel out of whack. So what have I learned on this journey?

The book topics have grown in number over the last three years. Some of the topics are also non-existent. This tells me that my interests are shifting. Hopefully the shifts add up to growth.

To me the blog serves as a depository of things I learn and wish to capture for future use. I share these with the world but the knowledge capture is truly for me. I want to be able to pick up my own books and refresh myself on the knowledge I obtained.

Of course I believe that the posts are valuable to others and that if a person is to pick up the three books, which are based on the blog, they will get a hack of an enlightenment in the topics that it covers. The books are more organized and edited and therefore more enjoyable to read.

I am also very thankful for the support and regular readers. The learning is personal but the sharing is the value that I believe I bring to my readers.

Enjoy

Robert Trajkovski

August 29,2014

www.ingramcontent.com/pod-product-compliance
Lightning Source LLC
LaVergne TN
LVHW051540070426
835507LV00021B/2342